PARTITION

PARTITION

HOW AND WHY IRELAND WAS DIVIDED

IVAN GIBBONS

This first paperback edition published in 2022

First published in 2020 by
HAUS PUBLISHING LTD
4 Cinnamon Row
London SW11 3TW

Sections of this book first appeared under the title *Drawing the Line* in
Haus Publishing's pamphlet series, the Haus Curiosities, in 2018.

Cartography produced by ML Design
Maps contain ordnance survey data
© Crown Copyright and Database Right 2011

ISBN: 978-1-913368-45-6
eISBN 978-1-913368-02-9

Typeset in Garamond by MacGuru Ltd

Printed in the United Kingdom by Clays Ltd, Elcograf S.p.A.

www.hauspublishing.com
@HausPublishing

For my sister, Virginia

Thanks to Hilda for all her advice and support

Contents

Preface   ix

Introduction   1
1. Ireland at the Beginning of the Twentieth Century   15
2. The Third Home Rule Act and the First World War   30
3. The Government of Ireland Act 1920   45
4. The Anglo-Irish Treaty   59
5. The Politics of the Irish Boundary Commission   79
6. The Recommendations of the Irish Boundary
    Commission   95
7. Aftermath   122

Suggested Further Reading   151
Chronology   154
Dramatis Personae   156
Index   162

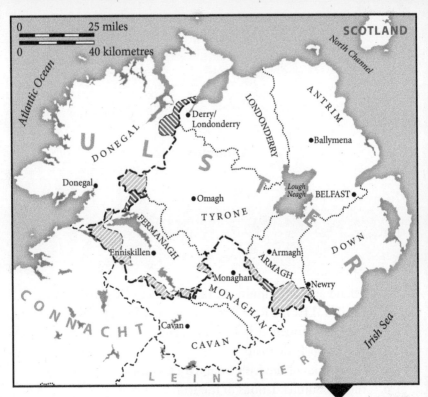

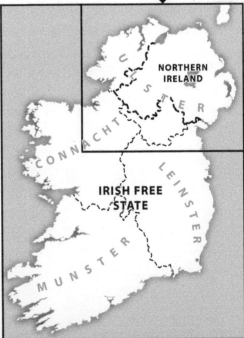

KEY

- –––– Boundary of 1920 Act

- ------ Boundary adjustments proposed by the 1925 Irish Boundary Commission

- ----- Province boundaries

- ·········· County boundaries

Proposed territorial changes

 From Northern Ireland to Irish Free State

From Irish Free State to Northern Ireland

LEINSTER Province of Ireland

TYRONE County

Preface

In the time since this book was first published – during the centenary of Ireland's partition – Northern Ireland has experienced considerable trauma. This is hardly the climate in which unionist politicians hoped to be celebrating the anniversary, which is significant in the history of not only Northern Ireland but the rest of Ireland too.

Demographic changes in Northern Ireland over the last several years indicate that the number of nationalists, most of whom have traditionally sought the reunification of Ireland, now approximates to the number of unionists seeking to maintain the constitutional link with Great Britain. In the 2011 census, 45% of the population of Northern Ireland specified they were Catholic, while 49% indicated they were from a Protestant background. These figures will almost certainly have narrowed by the time the results of the 2021 census are published. This is the exact opposite of why Northern Ireland was established one hundred years ago, which was to create a secure, inbuilt unionist majority in order to ensure that the north-east of Ireland – the unionist heartland – would remain a permanent part of the United Kingdom. Still, we cannot automatically assume that religious and political affiliation are always exactly the same in Northern Ireland. For example, whereas the vast majority of Protestants in Northern Ireland are invariably unionist in political outlook, recent surveys indicate that a substantial number of Catholics, while ostensibly nationalist, are prepared to accept or at least acquiesce in the existing constitutional status of Northern Ireland remaining part of the United Kingdom. The 2011 census results also indicate that, in that year, 40% considered themselves British only, 25% considered themselves Irish only, and 21% felt Northern Irish only. Others specified multiple national identities.

These census returns alone do not indicate that unionism is going through an existential crisis that will inevitably lead to a united Ireland in the medium-to-long-term future. Yet despite this, unionism (and more specifically loyalism or working-class unionism) is currently experiencing a severe crisis of confidence. Recent political developments – such as the implosion of the largest unionist party, the Democratic Unionist Party, and the psychological blow of the Brexit-inspired 'Northern Ireland Protocol' apparently breaching the link with the rest of the United Kingdom – have been fundamentally destabilising. Such political and economic uncertainty, which has questioned Northern Ireland's status in the United Kingdom, has also recently renewed rioting in working-class loyalist areas as well as unionist threats to collapse the power-sharing political structures at Stormont and thus once again threaten to undermine the Good Friday Agreement.

But to arrive at any conclusions now would be premature. Despite the current post-Brexit coolness in the relationship between the United Kingdom and the Republic of Ireland, there is little to indicate that both parties would welcome a politically destabilising border poll on the constitutional future of Northern Ireland in the immediate future. Even if one were proposed (and only the British government has the power to call one, according to the Good Friday Agreement), the outcome is uncertain. We must also await the outcome of the next Northern Ireland Assembly elections, scheduled to take place on or before 5 May 2022, to find out whether the existing political entity, created by partition in 1921, is going to enter its second century more or less stable than it is at present.

Introduction

The fact that partition was the single most important event in the history of the island of Ireland during the course of the twentieth century has, surprisingly, been downplayed by many Irish historians – Professor Ronan Fanning even went so far as to dismiss it as a story 'well known and soon told'.

As a historian teaching Irish history to university and adult education students in London, I always noticed a certain diffidence and reluctance to discuss the implications and consequences of this event in Irish history, the centenary of which we are commemorating. I wondered if this was because the Troubles in Northern Ireland of the late twentieth century were caused by, or, at least, heavily influenced by, this controversial event. I also noticed that students from Northern Ireland were far more ready to talk about the border than their fellow students from the south. Was there an element of guilt about how the south had allegedly abandoned the north all those years ago? It was clear that the drawing of the border was still a very raw event in the minds of so many Irish people. The occasion of its centenary in 2021 gave us an opportunity to learn about the story behind this momentous event, one that has so influenced Anglo-Irish relations for many decades.

Over almost forty years of teaching, I have always admired particularly those adult education students who, on a purely voluntary basis, came to learn more about Ireland and its relationship with Britain at a time when it wasn't always popular in this country to identify as Irish or want to know more about Ireland. I often wondered what the students' motivations were. In the case of those with no obvious link to Ireland it was more straightforward than it was for those with some Irish connection – a genuine attempt to understand the historical background to the story behind the news headlines. Each time something new was learned the inevitable comment was that they just hadn't been taught any of this at school!

The response of Irish-born students and those with Irish connections was far more nuanced. Most were there because they wanted to know more about their country, learning together with similar-minded Irish people at a time when it was problematic, to say the least, for many people to be Irish and living in London, despite the fact that, in most cases, they had made their whole lives there.

However, as central an event as partition was in Ireland, it is also immensely important in a wider context as Ireland's contribution to the great post-First World War upheavals in Europe (the partition proposal in the Anglo-Irish Treaty in 1921 appeared at the same time as the debate over how to divide Silesia between Germany and Poland). Ireland was not the only European country to be carved up in the tumultuous period after 1918. The fashionable political concept at the Treaty of Versailles, the peace agreement that concluded the First World War, was that of 'self-determination'. But attempting to untangle the varied political and national mix in the north of Ireland proved as problematic as attempting to do the same in central and eastern Europe. Silesia and East Prussia were as difficult to resolve as Ulster, and efforts to do so contained the seeds for future conflict.

Ireland was also the first of the partition proposals to be implemented in the subsequent decolonisation of the British Empire where, in the cases of India and Palestine, Ireland's example was seen as a suitable constitutional example to be followed. The British Empire had traditionally operated a successful policy when confronted with potential or actual conflict between continued membership of the Empire and the desire for self-determination of the peoples therein. This involved applying a full measure of self-government inside a federal structure, which seemed to have worked well in Canada and South Africa. But in cases of conflicting allegiances and national identities where competing claims for self-determination collided with each other – such as in Ireland, India and Palestine – the system began to break down. Partition was not the first choice of the British government in any of these cases. There is no evidence that Britain had a prepared divide-and-rule partitionist agenda for which Ireland was the template and which it found intrinsically attractive and was prepared to implement automatically. Indeed, there is evidence in all these cases that Britain would have preferred to have implemented alternative solutions but was defeated by the sheer acceleration of events and fear of the possible consequences of an unpredictable outcome to these developments.

The partition of Ireland was also part of the great debate as to the future constitutional composition of the United

Kingdom at the beginning of the twentieth century. Time has erased, or at least diluted, the memories of the tumultuous opening decades of the last century in Ireland. The south has metamorphosed into today's secular sovereign European state, while in the north the politics of parity of esteem has changed the former unionist province into, theoretically at least, a model of democratic power-sharing. But the border remains the border a century on, and the tensions, emotions and sensitivities that led to its creation are as powerful today as they were a hundred years ago.

Partition, or the threat of partition, had been part of the political background in Ireland ever since Irish nationalism began to assert itself in the late nineteenth century. The threat of loosening, or even removing, constitutional links with Britain was always going to attract an adverse reaction from Irish unionists, particularly those concentrated in numbers in the north-east of the country. Partition only became an overt and controversial political issue following the introduction of the Third Home Rule Bill in 1912; it had not featured at the time of the First Home Rule Bill in 1886 or the Second Home Rule Bill in 1893 – mainly because these had been defeated with relative ease at Westminster, the first in the Commons and the second in the Lords. However, it was already apparent by the 1880s that nationalist Ireland's growing desire for autonomy posed an increasing threat to the constitutional framework of the existing United Kingdom. Opponents of William Gladstone's commitment to Irish self-government argued that only a federal United Kingdom could prevent the potential constitutional dislocation that might be triggered by the introduction of a separate political structure created solely to satisfy Irish nationalist demands. Essentially, granting Home Rule to Ireland would create what became known over a century later during the debate on Scottish and Welsh devolution as the 'West Lothian question': bestowing upon a region of the United Kingdom, in this case Ireland, a parliament of its own while retaining that region's parliamentary presence at Westminster would give Ireland the right to vote on the internal affairs of England, Scotland and Wales without those countries being able to vote on internal Irish affairs. Gladstone's solution was to curtail Irish representation at Westminster, but to his opponents on the Home Rule issue, such as Joseph Chamberlain, this would mean that consequently Ireland would no longer have equal status inside the United Kingdom. To Chamberlain the ideal solution was to apply the federal model of Canada across the United Kingdom as an alternative to Home Rule in just one part; otherwise Gladstone was simply giving priority to Irish national grievances over social grievances in England and Scotland. Confronted with Irish Home Rule in the 1880s, Chamberlain preferred a proposed British federation with subordinate parliaments in Edinburgh, Cardiff, Dublin and, because of unionist opposition to rule from Dublin, Belfast as well. This would involve strictly demarcated roles with Westminster responsible for foreign affairs, defence, post office and customs, with the regional assemblies responsible for the rest.

A federalist reordering of the United Kingdom became a feature of British politics in the early twentieth century as Irish Home Rule became increasingly likely. The basic weakness of the concept, however, was the overwhelming status of England, both in terms of population and area, overshadowing Ireland, Scotland and Wales. Furthermore, apart from in Ireland, there was little popular support for such devolution, and ultimately the concept was dropped. The vestiges of the British federal idea can be seen in the Government of Ireland Act, intended originally as the first step in initiating such a project. It is interesting to speculate whether or not a federal reordering of the United Kingdom at an early enough stage could have maintained its constitutional integrity. The problem was that as soon as Home Rule for Ireland stopped dominating British politics the pressure for consideration of a federalist approach completely disappeared. There was also the uncomfortable fact that the federalists failed to pay much attention to, which was that Ireland was different and didn't fit neatly into this proposed constitutional reordering of the United Kingdom. As David Lloyd George famously said, 'Union – there is no union. There is union between Scotland and England and Wales. There is no union with Ireland. A grappling hook is not a union.'*

As it was, partition as a solution to the conflict of nationality in Ireland appeared as a realistic proposal in 1912 and started to gain traction during and after the First World War. The remote possibility of Irish unionism ever managing to reach an accommodation with the disciples of Irish Home Rule disappeared completely after the 1916 Easter Rising. Unionists interpreted this as a nefarious and treasonable nationalist plot to attack the country at a time of war. The political rift in Ireland became permanent when, in the aftermath of the

---

* House of Commons, Hansard, 31 March 1920, vol. 127, cols 1323–35.

uprising, the nationalism of imperial Irish Home Rulers was replaced by that of republican separatists. Indeed, Irish nationalism always had the option to offer a more ameliorating version of self-government with which to attract their Ulster Protestant fellow-countrymen but seemed consistently to replace moderate nationalism with more extreme versions, all of them guaranteed to repel unionism and accelerate the demand for partition.

However, we need to be wary of applying hindsight to the political situation that rapidly unfolded in Ireland in the decade between 1912 and 1922. Partition was not inevitable: the Third Home Rule Bill of 1912–14 did not inexorably lead to partition in 1921 or the establishment of two political entities in Ireland shortly afterwards. Although some evidence shows that James Craig, Edward Carson and the Ulster unionists had set the political goal of separating six Ulster counties from the rest of Ireland as early as 1913, this proposal was not initially shared widely beyond Protestant Ulster. Asquith's Liberal government was ostensibly committed to Home Rule for the whole of Ireland, while the Conservative opposition was against it. This was hardly surprising given the party's close political links and family ties with southern Irish unionists.

The 1916 Easter Rising and nationalist Ireland's subsequent endorsement of militant republicanism at the 1918 general election changed all that. If Ulster unionists in particular were unwilling to compromise with the moderate imperial nationalists led by John Redmond in the Irish Parliamentary Party – whose aim was an Ireland inside the British Empire with the same rights and freedoms as Canada and Australia – they were hardly likely to acquiesce in the revolutionary republicanism of Sinn Féin.

Partition became more likely after 1916 and almost certain after 1918. But, as the First World War ended, it wasn't just rapidly moving political developments in Ireland that facilitated partition. The war also saw a radical realignment in British politics, and it was shift that profoundly influenced events in Ireland. When Britain entered the war in 1914, it was governed by an exclusively Liberal government (the last ever Liberal government to date). This changed in December 1916, when the Liberal Lloyd George ditched his leader – Prime Minister Herbert Asquith – and entered a coalition government which, although led by Lloyd George, was dominated by the Conservatives. This was followed by the general election in 1918, in which Lloyd George was re-elected but at the head of another overwhelmingly Conservative coalition government. In the space of four years, Britain had moved from a Home Rule-supporting Liberal government to one wholly sympathetic to the demands of Ulster unionists. It was arguably this, not events in Ireland, that led to the partition of Ireland.

These dramatic changes have been neglected in explaining what happened in Ireland as the United Kingdom, after triumphing in a four-year war, lost one-fifth of its territory – more than the defeated German Empire. The partition of Ireland and the subsequent secession of what became the Irish Free State was also the partition of the United Kingdom. Yet there was little public disquiet about this in Britain. Why did British political parties and public opinion so quickly become disinterested in Ireland to the point that the support and sympathy for Ulster unionists that had characterised the British establishment's attitude to Ireland before the war had evaporated so much so that, after the war, it was of interest only to the right wing of the Conservative Party?

Undoubtedly, each British political party has to bear its share of responsibility for the eventual partition of Ireland. Despite its ideological affinity with Irish and, later, Ulster unionism and their shared belief in Crown, religion and empire, the British Conservative Party seized upon unionist intransigence to the possibility of Home Rule as a stick with which to beat their Liberal rivals at a time when the Tories had lost three general elections in a row and seemed unlikely to win one in the near future. Conservative support for Irish unionism from 1912 onwards seemed to be as opportunistic as Lord Randolph Churchill's playing of the 'Orange Card', that is cultivating for party political advantage Ulster Protestant fears and prejudices. It is reasonable to assume that, without this Conservative support, Ulster unionism would not have become the obdurate and intransigent force it did during and after the First World War.

If the Conservative Party can be criticised for its over-enthusiastic support for unionism, the British Liberal Party can be criticised for the exact opposite – espousing, however reluctantly, the growing demands of Irish nationalism, again for reasons of British party-political advantage, that is, to be able to form a government. The problem was that the Liberals only supported Irish nationalism weakly and half-heartedly backed Home Rule until Herbert Asquith was overthrown by Lloyd George. Irish Home Rule was ultimately sacrificed by Lloyd George's subsequent Conservative-dominated coalition government. In a pretty similar scenario, British Labour gave theoretical support to the principles of Irish self-rule but were more concerned with demonstrating their loyalty and fitness to govern in their new role in the early 1920s as Britain's official opposition party. Labour in government for the first time in 1924 was more determined to prove its responsibility in power than it ever was with promoting the aims of Irish self-determination.

Although it was obvious that there were competing nationalisms in Ireland dating back at least to the First Home Rule Bill, partition was not the inevitable outcome. In the months leading up to the outbreak of the First World War, there was very real concern in both Ireland and the rest of the United Kingdom that civil war rather than partition was the threat in Ulster. If this had happened and the Ulster Volunteers were victorious, there is every likelihood that there would have been a substantial Catholic refugee exodus and the creation of a smaller but more Protestant Ulster; conversely, if the Irish Volunteers had won, there would have been considerable Protestant flight to Scotland and England. Partition was a messy, pragmatic and second-best solution for all concerned, but it was one that avoided mass civil strife and the resulting refugee crisis.

For five years after it was defined in the Government of Ireland Act in 1920 up until the Tripartite Agreement of 1925, which ratified the border, partition was an ethereal concept – confirmed officially in legislation and on the map but impossible to trace in any tangible way. Ironically, many people only began to experience its impact once the Free State introduced customs controls in 1923. Of all the steps taken a hundred years ago to attempt to deal with Irish political turbulence, partition and the establishment of the border remains the most emotive. During the controversy since 2016 of Brexit and the so-called backstop,* there were many nationalist claims that the border, rather than being Irish, was, in fact, a British border in Ireland as Ireland's natural borders were the sea. This environmental determinism is exactly what Free State minister Ernest Blythe was trying to demolish in the 1920s when he argued that the border in Ireland was not imposed by the British but was the very obvious manifestation of the political reality that the two communities living in Ireland simply could not agree on a way forward politically and that nationalist Ireland had made very little effort to attract its unionist neighbours to its way of thinking.

Be that as it may, this did not mean that, once official, the border had to remain forever. Most of its friends and all its enemies would have been amazed to discover that it still exists a hundred years on. Realistically, there was perhaps a ten-year period during which the border could have been altered or even removed. I would suggest 1932 as the critical year. The border had just had its tenth anniversary, and its future was still debatable.

It was the continued uncertainty surrounding the permanence of partition that contributed substantially to Northern Ireland remaining such a paranoid political entity in the early years of its existence. To Ulster Unionists, the permanence

---

* The proposal that some aspects of the single market would be temporarily retained in Northern Ireland to avoid a hard border with the Republic of Ireland. The 'backstop' referred to the fact that this agreement could continue indefinitely if the UK did not agree alternative terms with the EU.

of partition was in doubt until the demise of the Boundary Commission in 1925. This paranoia and uncertainty must have been at least partly responsible for the outbreak of sectarian savagery in the north between 1920 and 1922. Bolstered by continuing violence in the south in the early years and backed by a British-financed security system, this was the period in which a confident and magnanimous unionist leadership could have shown the steadfastness and courage it employed in setting up the state to now reach out to the one-third of its population who were not unionist – but it didn't work out that way. The qualities that Sir James Craig exhibited in setting up Northern Ireland were not the same qualities he needed to employ to run his new fiefdom, in which every concession to Catholics was seen as a sign of weakness and surrender by so many unionists. Somebody like the aristocratic and patrician Lord Londonderry – the north's education minister, who tried to secularise education in 1923 and who acted as a check on Craig's increasingly sectarian, partisan and survivalist government – would have been a better candidate in any attempt to encourage Catholics to accept the existence of Northern Ireland. This would have involved taking their seats in the parliament and accommodating themselves to the unionist state. Instead, arrests, intimidation and internment, allied to the Free State's reluctance to recognise Northern Ireland, prevented nationalist MPs from entering parliament until the south climbed down after the Boundary Commission had run its course in 1925. In 1932 the leading nationalist politician in the north, Joseph 'Wee Joe' Devlin, stood down from Stormont, recognising the pointlessness of nationalist participation in the new unionist state. The opportunity of attracting the support, or at least the acquiescence, of Catholics to the reality of the new state had passed.

At the same time in the south, the irredentist republican Éamon de Valera won power, and the first pro-Treaty Free State government was defeated. De Valera's resolute non-recognition of Northern Ireland was instrumental in northern nationalist MPs refusing to participate in its parliament. Although the Free State was adept at introducing Catholic principles into social and cultural legislation right from its inception, it was de Valera who benefited most politically from the holding of the 31st International Eucharistic Congress* in Dublin in June 1932. This emphasis on the Catholic history and nature of the Free State inevitably entrenched partition more deeply, and, although not seen as a threat to or by northern Protestants, was merely an inevitable confirmation of the nature of the Free State. In its support for Catholic triumphalism and its implied exclusion of non-Catholics, the Irish Free State was increasingly becoming a Catholic state. 1932 was also the year that saw the start of the Anglo-Irish Trade War,† thus once more ramping up tension with Ireland's nearest neighbour and major trading partner and creating further antagonism with the north.

In Britain, the Labour government had resigned as a result of the economic collapse caused by the Great Depression. It was replaced in 1931 by a national government led by Ramsay

---

* A large, week-long religious Catholic gathering.

† Also known as the Economic War, the Anglo-Irish Trade War involved unilateral trade restrictions on the part of both countries as a result of de Valera's government refusing to repay sums lent by successive British governments to Irish tenant farmers by various pre-independence land acts.

MacDonald and Stanley Baldwin, the two British politicians who most wanted Ireland removed from any involvement in British politics. Those politicians most indifferent to Ireland would now be in charge of Britain for the next five years. Furthermore, the Statute of Westminster approved at the Commonwealth Conference in 1931 gave each Dominion equal status and legislative independence and thus enabled de Valera to legitimately and peacefully remove most of the constitutional links between Ireland and the British Crown.

Without exception, all of these developments solidified and underpinned partition. With a different set of circumstances in the period 1922–32, it might have been possible to have a rapprochement between some or all of those involved. This would not necessarily have led to the end of partition – in fact, it probably wouldn't have – but for those who wanted to see the end of partition in Ireland, this period, during which relationships between the major players were in flux, was the best opportunity to achieve it. Once that opportunity had been lost, it is perhaps not surprising that partition continued to survive various vicissitudes throughout the rest of the century and is still in place today.

1

Ireland at the Beginning of the Twentieth Century

An eighty-year-old Queen Victoria disembarked at Kingstown (Dún Laoghaire) on the morning of 4 April 1900 to begin her fourth and final trip to Ireland. She had visited on three previous occasions in 1849, 1853 and 1861, but the Ireland she visited just nine months before she died in January 1901 was a very different country from the one she had visited much earlier in her reign.

Despite allegations that this visit was no more than a recruiting tool for the Boer War, the queen spent much of the three weeks she was in Dublin visiting Catholic institutions, such as schools and hospitals, including Castleknock College, Mount Anville Convent, Loreto Abbey, Rathfarnham and the Mater Hospital. She was also entertained by the Artane Boys Band in Phoenix Park. The visit to Castleknock was the first time that a British sovereign had ever visited an Irish Catholic college.

The Irish Catholic hierarchy had been lukewarm about the visit, and there were dire warnings in sections of the British press that she would meet a hostile reception, but there was no denying the enthusiasm that welcomed her to Dublin. To what extent this was genuine allegiance to the throne or merely ordinary Dublin Catholics having a day off and exhibiting non-political enjoyment of the grandeur, symbolism and spectacle of the monarchy is a moot point. The majority of Dublin's largely Catholic population was always drawn to such imperial events by a combination of spectacle, celebrity, affection, curiosity, loyalty and simple fun. Certainly, the visit highlighted the chasm between constitutional and radical Irish nationalists whose great fear was that such visits ran the risk of reconciling ordinary Catholics to the connection with Britain. Municipal nationalists in Dublin resented the popular enjoyment of such festivities, fearing any consolidation of royalist sentiment and the resultant confusion of nationalist aspirations.

Despite the fact that within a generation radical nationalists were to run Ireland, in 1900 they were regarded as marginal eccentrics by most of the Irish nationalist population. Even so, the authorities were careful not to highlight the fact that the royal visit in 1900 was taking place on the centenary of the Act of Union, which incorporated Ireland into the British United Kingdom. This was probably a wise decision, as any such demonstration of what could be interpreted as triumphalism would have run the very real risk of reopening what appeared to be recently healed political sores.

It was an act of faith amongst all Irish nationalists that the Act of Union was the source of all Ireland's ills throughout the nineteenth century. Even William Pitt, the author of the Act of Union, knew that ruling Ireland directly from Westminster would solve nothing. The union of Great Britain and Ireland was politically expedient in the middle of the Napoleonic Wars as a response to the very real threat of French republicanism overwhelming Ireland during the 1798 rebellion against British control. It achieved very little and certainly did not solve the Irish grievances over land, religion and politics that had been festering since the seventeenth century. The stark reality was that an industrialising Britain in the early nineteenth century had failed to incorporate an old-fashioned agricultural economy such as Ireland into the new constitutional order.

Pitt, rather, knew that social and economic reforms were essential, as was Catholic Emancipation. The Act of Union was hobbled at birth as the subsequent expectation that Catholic Emancipation would soon follow – which had persuaded the Catholic hierarchy to support (or at least acquiesce in) the union – was immediately dashed when George III refused to support it, believing it to be in breach of his coronation oath to uphold the Anglican Church. Pitt – who knew that the refusal to countenance any social and political progress, including Catholic Emancipation, would be detrimental to the future success of the union between the two countries – resigned in protest. The Act of Union now became a political liability rather than a harbinger of a new and equal relationship between the two islands. At the beginning of the nineteenth century, when anti-Catholic prejudice was still rife in Britain, the prospect of a rapidly growing Irish Catholic population effectively outnumbering British Protestants in the new United Kingdom at a time when Ireland's population was four million and Britain's was only ten million implied, it was believed by many British and Irish Protestants, a very real threat to the status quo. This British anti-Catholic patriotic zeal stopped Catholic Emancipation in its tracks and ended all Pitt's intended reforms.

It is one of the what-might-have-beens of Anglo-Irish history: what if Irish Roman Catholics had been welcomed into the new United Kingdom as full and equal citizens? As it was, the situation continued to deteriorate. When Catholic Emancipation was eventually granted in 1829, it was done so reluctantly under the implied threat of political violence and anarchy if the demands of Daniel O'Connell's emancipation campaign were not satisfied. An attempt by O'Connell to revive his flagging political popularity by employing the same tactics in a campaign to repeal the Act of Union in the 1840s was less successful, perhaps unsurprisingly at a time when a substantial proportion of Catholic Ireland was more concerned with survival during the Great Famine than with constitutional reform. As it was, the famine was regarded in nationalist Irish folklore as yet another consequence of the union – despite the fact that the economic circumstances causing it pre-dated the event by at least a century.

It is significant that when an assertive Irish nationalism began to manifest itself in the final quarter of the nineteenth century, uniting economic and political grievances under the charismatic leadership of Charles Stewart Parnell in the Irish Home Rule movement, it was not to achieve total separation from Britain through the repeal of the hated Act of Union but merely to secure limited self-government inside the United Kingdom. However, even this modest amount of self-determination proved anathema to the Protestant and increasingly unionist population, particularly those concentrated geographically in the north-east. This section of the Irish population had political and economic interests diametrically opposite to those of the rest of the country. Whereas nationalist Ireland held the Act of Union directly responsible for its economic and political malaise – from the decline of Dublin as a national capital to its status as a provincial backwater right through to the Great Famine and the hobbling of Irish industry and indeed any economic development deemed to be a rival to that of Britain's – so Ireland's (and in particular Ulster's) unionist population believed exactly the opposite. To them, the Act of Union opened the gateway to the markets and raw materials of the emerging British Empire, which would fuel the expansion of Ulster's growing industrial might concentrated on shipbuilding, linen and heavy industry.

Ireland's unionists repeatedly pointed out, with some historical justification, that Ireland had only ever been politically united under British central authority, whether monarchical or parliamentarian. Although the first two Home Rule Bills were pretty easily defeated in parliament (in 1886 in the House of Commons and in 1893 in the House of Lords) without any recourse to, or promises of, special treatment for the unionist heartland of the north-east, there were some harbingers of what impact the threat or likelihood of a successful Home Rule movement could have on Ireland as a single political entity. First, the reluctance of unionists even to consider a modest and minimal amount of local self-government did not augur well for the future when Home Rule faced the very real possibility of becoming a political reality, let alone a political scenario in the future when the drivers of Irish national demands were not the moderate constitutional Home Rulers but the revolutionary republicans with their tactics of extra-parliamentary violence. Although talk of secession or partition was a long way off, it was becoming apparent by the time of the

Home Rule controversies that the most effective opposition to self-government would emanate from that part of the country where the Protestant unionists were demographically strong. Already, Liberal Unionists at Westminster such as Joseph Chamberlain were speculating about a form of partition with the application of federalism inside the United Kingdom with an additional parliament at Belfast as the solution to the conflict of nationalities in Ireland. Even as long ago as the 1840s, during the debates on the proposed repeal of the Act of Union, the Whig historian and politician Lord Macaulay had argued that O'Connell's justification for a separate Irish parliament in Dublin could logically be countered by a proposal to have a parliament for Ulster in the city of Derry/Londonderry* given its symbolism for a separate Ulster Protestant identity going back to the seventeenth century.

The early Home Rule Bills and the unionist rejection of them emphasised the growth of a separate Ulster Protestant identity, not necessarily a non-Irish one (certainly not at this stage) but one determined to maintain Ireland's or, increasingly, Ulster's constitutional position inside the United Kingdom. It also led directly to the foundation of a separate Irish Unionist party in 1891 and a suspicion of both of the mainstream British political parties when Irish unionism discovered that Salisbury's Conservatives had entered into negotiations with Parnell's Home Rulers following the outcome of the inconclusive 1885 general election.

However, as the twentieth century dawned, the political

---

* The city's name has a controversial history: Derry is the nationalist term and Londonderry the unionist term. Hereafter, the city will be referred to as Derry.

climate in Ireland had calmed. The Liberal split over Home Rule in 1886 ushered in a period of nearly twenty years' uninterrupted Conservative government until 1906, save for a brief return by Gladstone and the Liberals from 1892 to 1895. Home Rule had been defeated twice, the Home Rule movement split over the leadership of Parnell in 1890, and from 1895 to 1905 the Conservative government introduced a policy of what was called 'constructive unionism'. This involved ploughing tens of thousands of pounds into public works, particularly in the impoverished areas known as 'congested districts' in the west of Ireland, while funding the compulsory purchase of rural land from landowners in order to compensate small farmers. Constructive unionism, also referred to as 'killing Home Rule by kindness', was often accompanied by a tough security policy, but it was a genuine, if pragmatic, attempt to utilise public investment to tackle poverty and undermine economic grievance, the greatest being the unresolved land question. The building of railways and harbours in the west of Ireland immeasurably improved the lot of previously politically sullen and disgruntled poverty-stricken rural Irish. The allocation of Congested Districts Board* funds also stimulated private investment in railways and other infrastructure. Apocryphal stories – such as the young women of Creeslough in Co. Donegal no longer having to give their confessions to their local prying parish priest now that they could take the recently built Londonderry and Lough Swilly Railway to the

---

* Established by Arthur Balfour when he was Chief Secretary to Ireland in 1891, the Congested Districts Boards provided funding to improve living conditions in impoverished parts of west and north-west Ireland.

neighbouring parishes of Falcarragh and Dunfanaghy – illustrated the very real wider social and economic opportunities introduced into previously remote and isolated parts of the west of Ireland through the investment of the Congested Districts Board. However, what constructive unionism failed to keep abreast of was the growth in cultural nationalism in Ireland in the late nineteenth century.

Home Rule retreated from the political stage after 1893 to be followed by the Conservative effort to address Catholic and nationalist grievances in areas such as land ownership, local government and education and to reduce emigration through job creation. The undermining of the landed classes led to a process of Ulsterisation, in which the leadership of unionism moved from southern landlords to the northern commercial and industrial middle classes. This group of young middle-class unionists felt that the Conservatives were ignoring their interests and that the landed Anglo-Irish elite no longer had the necessary social and political influence it once held. Consequently, the Ulster Unionist Council was formed in 1905. This would provide the basis for unionist opposition to Home Rule between 1912 and 1914 and would be the originating force behind partition. In other words, the victory that British unionism conceded to the largely Catholic and nationalist Irish tenantry through their land purchase and redistribution policy tilted the balance of leadership within Irish unionism decisively from south to north by transferring power and influence from the Protestant landed class to the unionist commercial class and ultimately facilitated partition. The Local Government (Ireland) Act of 1898, which democratised local government, and Wyndham's Land Act of

1903, which reversed the seventeenth-century land confiscations, both initiated the greatest social revolution in Ireland in centuries and pre-dated Ireland's political revolution by a generation. The availability of British-government funds for Irish land transfers made the sale of smallholdings and even whole estates profitable to landlords while guaranteeing purchase terms that tenant farmers could meet. This erosion of Protestant economic power in rural Ireland was matched by the removal of their political power, and all of this was achieved twenty-five years before Ireland acquired its own government.

The Ireland that Queen Victoria visited in 1900, then, was at its calmest politically than it had been for a decade. The apparent collapse of Home Rule, the decline and death of Parnell – the foremost nationalist politician of his generation, the consequent split in the Irish Parliamentary Party only resolving in 1900 under the leadership of John Redmond – and the impotence of the Home Rulers in this period of political disarray and disunity of purpose led many young Irish nationalists to turn instead to the new cultural and militant movements and also enabled the Catholic clergy to fill the political vacuum. The removal of the land issue as the overriding source of economic grievance, the democratisation of Irish local government so that Catholics were now in charge in most of the country outside the north-east and the relative success of the Congested Districts Board (although there was criticism that it gave undue influence to the Catholic Church as it was administered by parish priests and could be wasteful and profligate) all contributed towards lowering the political temperature in turn-of-the-twentieth-century Ireland. Fenian bomb outrages, whether in Ireland or Britain, had long since ceased, and it seemed that even the underground recruitment and infiltration of cultural organisations such as the Gaelic Athletic Association by the Irish Republican Brotherhood was more of an irritant than anything else. Even the renowned cultural revival seemed just that: a cultural phenomenon with very little political significance.

In the early years of the twentieth century there appeared little likelihood of Home Rule reaching the statute book. As a result of previous Home Rule Bills having been comprehensively defeated, the Liberal Party was wary of remaining associated with a failed policy that consumed so much parliamentary time and effort. Furthermore, Home Rule was exclusively associated with one man in the Liberal Party – Gladstone – and when he departed from the political stage in 1895 there was no surviving legacy inside the party that embraced Home Rule ideologically in the way, for example, that Andrew Bonar Law did with unionism inside the Conservative Party. However, there was another, more fundamental impediment to Home Rule being implemented: in order for it to happen, the Liberal Party had to start winning elections – and even then it would have to find itself dependent on Irish Home Rulers at Westminster. The Liberals lost the 1900 general election in the great patriotic surge during the Boer War which gave the Conservatives a substantial majority. It won in the massive Liberal landslide of 1906, but, unfortunately (from a Home Rule perspective), the Liberals were just too successful and did not have to depend on Irish nationalist MPs to form a government; that only happened after the two inconclusive general election results in 1910.

So, in the first decade of the twentieth century, Home Rule remained the ultimate ambition – the Holy Grail – of Irish nationalists, but it was unlikely to be achieved in the foreseeable future. Irish nationalist politicians therefore settled into a pattern of enjoying the electoral benefits of democratic reform of the local government system which, far-sightedly, had enfranchised Irish workers and women in 1898. Ever since the mid-nineteenth century there had been developing in Ireland an increasingly confident Catholic bourgeoisie, but now, in the early years of the twentieth century, this nationalist middle class was aware that demographically and democratically its time was about to come. Most local authorities in Ireland were now controlled by nationalists of one stripe or another. Given the overwhelming Catholic nature of the electorate outside of Ulster, there was little political opposition on these councils. This environment allowed for the development of a culture of complacency, and there were many examples of jobbery and corruption. Indeed, unionists used the example of the corruption prevalent in many nationalist-controlled councils to point out what would happen in Ireland as a whole if ever Home Rule were enacted. On Dublin City Council there developed an unlikely alliance between the ascetic nationalists of Sinn Féin and civic-minded unionists ever ready to highlight the perceived and actual decline in municipal standards as they unearthed examples of nationalist corruption on the Corporation, the Council's predecessor. The prevailing culture of malaise in much of Irish nationalist society at this time is clearly exemplified by novelist James Joyce in 'The Dead', the final short story in *Dubliners*, set in 1904. This story of tedium and paralysis is often portrayed as a powerful metaphor for the torpor permeating conventional society both socially and politically in early-twentieth-century nationalist Ireland.

Meanwhile, the election in 1906 of a radical Liberal government that was dedicated to social reform made many Irish nationalists question their commitment to separation from Britain as the emergence of a proto-welfare state became a reality. The Liberals also completed the policy of land reform of the previous Conservative government when they financed forty thousand rural labourers to become proprietors of their own cottage homes. The introduction of old-age pensions, labour exchanges and national insurance (although it was not fully implemented in Ireland) as well as progressive labour legislation were attractive inducements to many Irish nationalists to remain part of a more prosperous United Kingdom – so much so that Tom Clarke, one of the leaders of the 1916 rising, felt impelled to persuade Patrick Pearse to make his rallying speech at the funeral of the old Fenian O'Donovan Rossa in 1915 a call to arms to the physical-force tradition of Irish republicanism. Both Clarke and, much later, Irish taoiseach Garret FitzGerald believed that the 1916 Easter Rising was a political necessity if Ireland were not to be finally and effectively incorporated totally into the United Kingdom. But many labour activists were also seduced by the prospect of a better standard of living in the United Kingdom. Although they remained nationalists – the Irish Labour Party being formed in 1912 to represent labour interests in a forthcoming Home Rule parliament – many were under no illusions that a Home Rule parliament, dominated as it would be by the Catholic bourgeoisie, would be sympathetic to Labour demands. Many Irish women were also deterred by the refusal of John Redmond and the Irish Parliamentary Party to support women's suffrage on the grounds that it would take up valuable parliamentary time needed for the implementation of Home Rule.

As it was, Home Rule was propelled back into the centre of Irish politics, not because of any upsurge in popularity or increased demand for such a measure in Ireland but because of the outcome of the two British general elections in 1910. The January election was held in the middle of a constitutional crisis triggered by the rejection of Lloyd George's People's Budget – which sought to fund a radical new social welfare programme through increased taxes on the wealthy – by the Conservative-dominated House of Lords. Both this election and the following one in December were called so that the Liberal government could secure a mandate to pass the budget. In the event, the Liberals were only able to form a government with the support of the Irish Parliamentary Party, whose price for that support was the introduction, after a gap of nearly twenty years, of yet another Home Rule Bill. The difference was that this latest Bill was likely to become law, as the recently enacted Parliament Act of 1911 had replaced the unlimited veto of the House of Lords with one lasting only three parliamentary sessions, meaning that a bill passed in the Commons could not be blocked by the Lords for longer than two years.

It was with a heavy heart that Liberal prime minister Herbert Asquith introduced the latest Home Rule Bill on 11 April 1912. Ireland was only one of many issues and problems requiring his energies, for, in addition to escalating industrial unrest and a growing militant suffragette campaign, the

Liberals were also occupied with implementing their massive social reform programme as well as accelerating an intensifying naval arms race with Germany. Asquith had been Home Secretary in Gladstone's final administration between 1892 and 1894 and had seen the inordinate amount of parliamentary time taken up trying to pilot the Second Home Rule Bill through the House of Commons. (The 1893 Bill still holds the record for having the largest amount of parliamentary time spent on debating a piece of proposed legislation.) There had been no commitment to Home Rule in the Liberal election manifesto in 1910, whereas opposition to the proposed measure had most definitely been in the Conservative manifesto. Home Rule was seen by most Liberal politicians as the last great obsession of Gladstonian Liberalism come back to haunt them twenty years on. Consequently, the Conservatives proved better allies for unionists than the Liberals ever were for the Home Rulers. Given the Liberals' apathy and lack of application to ensuring that Home Rule became a reality, it is curious that Irish nationalists never made any attempt to negotiate with the Tories in 1906 and 1910 in the same way that Parnell did with Salisbury in 1886.

The Government of Ireland Bill or Third Home Rule Bill, as introduced in 1912, was intended to establish Home Rule or self-government for Ireland within the United Kingdom. When it became law in 1914, it was the first time that parliament had sought to implement devolved government in any part of the kingdom. The Bill proposed a bicameral Irish parliament in Dublin consisting of 164 MPs and a forty-member senate, a consequent reduction of the number of Irish MPs at Westminster from 103 to forty and the abolition of the

British administration in Dublin Castle with the exception of the Lord-Lieutenant (the monarch's representative in Ireland). The Bill's preamble, however, also asserted the supreme authority of the United Kingdom's parliament 'over all persons, matters and things in Ireland'.

In nationalist Ireland, the reaction to the introduction of the Home Rule Bill was muted. Many nationalists regarded it as a relatively modest proposal, while radical separatist nationalists rejected it outright. Irish unionists began mobilising against it immediately, skilfully exploiting their carefully nurtured connections with the Conservative Party particularly after Bonar Law, with his Ulster ancestry, became Conservative Party leader in 1911. The Conservatives interpreted Home Rule as 'a corrupt political bargain'* that was being foisted upon the United Kingdom simply to keep the Liberals in power.

Even so, at the beginning of 1912 there was hardly a cataclysmic response in nationalist Ireland to the prospect of Home Rule becoming a reality. Even the most far-sighted political observer was unable to predict that in the course of the next decade Ireland would be divided into two states: one a self-governing Dominion outside the United Kingdom but inside the Empire, like Australia and Canada, and the other a devolved self-governing political unit remaining inside the United Kingdom. Our clairvoyant political observer would have been even less likely to foresee that this arrangement would continue, with the larger political unit in Ireland ultimately becoming a totally independent country, as the constitutional status quo for the next century.

---

* This phrase was used at a Unionist rally at Blenheim Palace in July 1913.

2

The Third Home Rule Act and the First World War

With the Liberal government dependent upon Irish Home Rule MPs after the two inconclusive general election results of 1910, Irish unionism, after a twenty-year hiatus, found itself once again in mortal danger. This time, however, the threat was more existential, as the unionists' previous final bulwark against the threat of Home Rule, the House of Lords' veto, had been abolished. With a hostile government once more, however reluctantly, committed to Home Rule, unionists were now without effective allies in parliament given that their Conservative allies were now in seemingly permanent opposition.

Furthermore, the Irish Parliamentary Party MPs at Westminster were mostly typical of the increasingly confident middle-class, middle-aged Catholic bourgeoisie that had grown to dominate Irish society and politics over the previous generation, but there was now another threat facing unionism. This was the new, assertive Irish nationalism of Irish-Irelandism, a potent combination of cultural, economic and political nationalism that had begun to attract younger and more radical nationalists during the recent period of political stasis when constitutional nationalism appeared to be paralysed and impotent. In a very short period this new approach would supplant Home Rule with a more vibrant and assertive nationalism – and it would pose a far greater threat to unionism than the Home Rulers ever did.

Irish nationalism had traditionally been a southern rural phenomenon. Most Irish nationalists rarely gave Irish unionism a second thought, and, if they did, it was to regard their fellow citizens – mostly concentrated in the north – as misguided or deluded in their political opinions. However, Irish nationalists were firm in their belief that, when the time came, most unionists would see the light and fall into line politically. The Irish-Irelanders, however, went one step further. Again, this was essentially a southern nationalist philosophy, which asserted that the essence of Irishness – Gaelic and Catholic – was the polar opposite of what Irish (and specifically Ulster) unionists cherished: their Britishness, the Empire, the monarchy and, above all, their Protestantism. This purist philosophy of Irishness fetishised the people, landscape, language and economy of the rural west of Ireland as harking back to a simpler age unsullied by the twin evils of modernity and materialism. Unfortunately, this was also the least developed and poorest part of the country, the exact opposite of what the urban, industrialised north had become over the previous century. To many Irish nationalists, Ulster and the majority of the people who lived there were foreign and non-Irish. To them Belfast was an alien British city in Ireland, more like Liverpool or Glasgow than Dublin, and it was routinely and pejoratively dismissed as the 'black north'.

But Irish unionism was not a homogenous entity. The unionism of the southern landed elite, now much reduced in political and social influence, was not that of the Belfast industrial working class. Indeed, the former differed substantially from the sophisticated, urban, professional middle class that characterised Protestant Dublin and Cork unionism. However, all agreed that an Ireland under Home Rule would be an Ireland dominated by the doctrines and values of the Roman Catholic hierarchy and clergy. In the north there were also sizeable labour and trade-union movements as well as a strong tradition of Presbyterian unionism. Although both movements and Presbyterianism ultimately agreed with the landed and bourgeois elements' belief that Ulster's future prosperity and wellbeing depended upon remaining part of the United Kingdom, they also remembered that their ancestors had in the previous century removed an Anglican ascendancy* and therefore had no intention of replacing it with a Roman Catholic one. In the north, in particular, the activities of the Ancient Order of Hibernians – which has been described as the Catholic version of the Orange Order[†] – in intertwining Home Rule politics with the interests of the Catholic Church appeared to these unionists to be an indicator of what a Home Rule Ireland would turn into.

Faced with such an existential threat, Ulster Protestants were fortunate that Sir Edward Carson had become unionist leader in 1910 and that Bonar Law, of Ulster Protestant ancestry himself, had replaced Arthur Balfour as Conservative

---

* Anglican, rather than Protestant, is used deliberately here as there had been historical tension between Anglicans and Presbyterians.

† A Protestant political society, deeply connected with Ulster loyalism. Once a secret society, the Orange Order is still known for marches that have been criticised as sectarian and triumphalist.

leader in 1911. Both Carson and Bonar Law exhibited the ideological commitment to the unionist case so obviously missing from the Liberal front bench with its lukewarm support for Home Rule. Both politicians believed that the threat of Home Rule would lead to the destruction of the United Kingdom and ultimately the entire British Empire. But whereas Bonar Law was ultimately an Ulster unionist, Carson was an Irish unionist from Dublin who hoped and believed that opposition to Home Rule in Ulster could prevent the granting of Home Rule to the whole of Ireland.

While their support for unionism in Ireland was genuine and sincere, the Tories also sensed a political opportunity. The Conservative Party had long regarded itself the natural party of government, but by 1912 it had been out of office for over five years and had experienced yet another philosophical split on the vexed issue of tariff reform* in 1910. However, in addition to their ideological affinity with the Irish unionists, the Conservatives knew that there was massive popular support in Britain for the Ulster unionists given the predicament in which they now found themselves. Furthermore, the Tories remembered that their adroit exploitation of British jingoism in the midst of the Boer War had resulted in their massive 'khaki election' victory – one heavily influenced by wartime patriotism – in 1900, and they hoped to propel themselves back into power by repeating that tactic, this time on the issue of Irish Home Rule. This would, however, require sensitivity on the part of Bonar Law as

---

*Tariff reform, as opposed to free trade, was a protectionist initiative that sought to 'protect' domestic industries through imposing duties on imports.

there were residual elements inside British Conservatism that had reservations about their party – committed as it was to upholding the constitution and law and order – consorting with the wilder elements of what they perceived as illegality and sectarianism in Ulster unionism. These reservations only increased when the more overt expressions of sectarian anti-Catholicism began to be articulated amongst the more extreme elements of their Ulster allies.

Despite increasing political instability in Ireland from April 1912, when Liberal prime minister Asquith introduced the Third Home Rule Bill – which led to the signing of the Ulster Covenant in September 1912 and the establishment of two rival paramilitary armies in Ireland, one unionist and one nationalist, both importing arms from Germany – Ulster unionists did not formally demand the partition of Ireland and the establishment of an Irish border until late 1913.

When Liberal backbencher Thomas Agar-Robartes moved an amendment to the Third Home Rule Bill in June 1912 proposing that the four most Protestant Ulster counties of Londonderry, Down, Antrim and Armagh should be excluded from the legislation, the response was like a scene from a Bateman cartoon – revulsion, disapprobation and outrage. Agar-Robartes was the first British politician to formally propose the partition of Ireland and the establishment of an Irish border. In doing so he unwittingly set in motion a process that was to have a profound political impact on the island of Ireland as well as its relationship with Britain up to the present day. His proposal was an attempt to respond to the growing opposition to Home Rule from, in particular, Ulster unionists, but even so, both British and Irish politicians, irrespective of party, regarded his proposal as an assault upon the constitutional and geographical integrity of both the United Kingdom and Ireland. When Agar-Robartes stood up in the House of Commons in June 1912 and called for the exclusion of four Ulster counties from Home Rule, he was proposing not only that Ireland be partitioned but that the historic province of Ulster be partitioned also. His proposal for the exclusion of the most Protestant counties also inevitably implied that the other five of the nine counties of Ulster were going to be 'abandoned' to Home Rule.

The philosophical principle underlying the Agar-Robartes proposal was that Ireland was two nations rather than one. Over the next eight years this became the unstated but logical argument of those who favoured partition, and, although this thesis could be (and frequently was) criticised intellectually, in the end it became a self-fulfilling prophecy. The Conservatives voted for the amendment, but this did not mean that they backed partition at this stage. They supported it purely for tactical reasons as, like Sir Edward Carson, they believed that it had the propensity to scupper the whole notion of Home Rule for the entire island.

For legislation that caused so much consternation both inside and outside parliament, the Third Home Rule Bill seemed disproportionately modest. It was modelled on Gladstone's Second Home Rule Bill of 1893 rather than the far more expansive proposals contained in the original Bill of 1886. The 1912 Bill excluded from the Dublin parliament's control – in addition to the expected imperial spheres of government such as war, naval and military affairs, treaties and foreign affairs – land purchase, old-age pensions, national insurance and post office savings banks. However, it was the principle of Home Rule that was anathema to the unionists and their Tory allies; the actual mechanics of the legislation were incidental.

Even before the Bill was introduced and shortly after the Parliament Act was passed in 1911, Carson and other leading unionists were bellicosely threatening to assume responsibility for Ulster by establishing their own provisional government. A well-drilled Protestant militia was set up, which very shortly would become the Ulster Volunteer Force (UVF). The entirety of Ulster unionism mobilised in resistance to the imminent passing of the Bill. The legislation was attacked on two fronts: parliamentary and extra-parliamentary. The Orange Order was put on alert for possible civil conflict, and Ulster unionist clubs were revived. A massive propaganda campaign was initiated in Britain, while Ulster saw a plethora of marches, speeches and rallies in Protestant towns and villages. In parliament, lengthy speeches and obstructive amendments were employed in an attempt to make the Liberal government think again. This was followed by the signing of the Ulster Solemn League and Covenant* by over half a million Ulster unionists and its presentation at Belfast City Hall in September 1912. In early 1913 the previously disparate Protestant militias totalling nearly one hundred thousand men were organised into the UVF, which then began to import arms from Germany. Finally, in late 1913, Ulster unionists demanded the introduction of partition and the establishment of a border in Ireland. They had quickly come to realise (as the southern unionists

---

* Often known simply as the Ulster Covenant, the Ulster Solemn League and Covenant was a document opposing Home Rule.

feared they would do sooner or later) that only the north (and not even all of that) could realistically be exempt from Home Rule. Their allies at Westminster, the Conservatives, now also accepted that the greater part of Ireland must be allowed to go its own way and that Ireland would have to be divided politically. The question then was how this was to be done. Asquith had always admitted during the course of parliamentary debates on Home Rule that ultimately special provision would have to be made to accommodate Ulster unionist opposition, but he was not prepared to indicate what that could be until Home Rule was on the statute book and had become the law of the land.

In the meantime, debate raged about exactly where the new Irish border should be. In 1914 this would, of course, not be an international border, as it would merely be dividing two areas that would both remain part of the United Kingdom with the northern, excluded part of Ireland simply remaining administered directly from Westminster.

Carson, as unionist leader, initially proposed the exclusion of the historic nine-county province of Ulster. As a Dublin-born southern unionist, Carson was in a difficult ideological position, as were the British Tories. Carson was the leader of all Irish unionists, and his initial encouragement of northern unionist intransigence was merely a device to derail the Home Rule proposal for all of Ireland. Although he remained as head of Irish unionism until 1921, Carson's long-term ambition of mobilising Ulster unionism in order to prevent the whole of Ireland leaving the United Kingdom had, in effect, perished in the months before the outbreak of the First World War. The fact that he was ultimately replaced by northern businessman and landowner Sir James Craig, who also became prime minister of the new Northern Ireland at the same time, was belated confirmation that unionist power and influence in Ireland had long ago passed from southern to northern unionists. Carson's career as Attorney General and First Lord of the Admiralty in the British wartime government and his membership of the War Cabinet as well as his continued defence of Ulster unionist interests could not disguise the fact that his overriding political ambition of maintaining all of Ireland inside the union had ended in total failure.

The Tories also recognised, pragmatically but realistically, that only that part of Ireland with a numerically strong Protestant and unionist population could be exempt from the new arrangements. From now on, all efforts would be devoted to maximising the number of unionists to be excluded from Home Rule while minimising the risk to the future viability of the excluded area by limiting nationalists inside that area to a number that could be tolerated from a demographic and security perspective.

It would have proven difficult if the entire province of Ulster, with more or less equal numbers of Catholics and Protestants, had become the excluded area. This would have been easier if London had remained responsible for security, but it would have been far more problematic once it was agreed, five years later, that a new state of Northern Ireland was to be created and it was to be responsible for its own security. Pragmatic Ulster unionists now realised that much of the historic province of Ulster and its longstanding Protestant population, surrounded by an overwhelming Catholic majority, would have to be surrendered to a nationalist-controlled

Ireland. The abandonment of their co-religionists in the Catholic-dominated Ulster border counties rankled, but the hurt was assuaged by Tyrone and Fermanagh, both counties with small Catholic majorities, being proposed for inclusion in the excluded area.

In the months before the outbreak of the First World War, and just before the Third Home Rule Bill reached the statute book, the Liberal government finally indicated what special provision for Ulster might consist of. Lloyd George had proposed on behalf of the government in late 1913 that the four most unionist counties – Antrim, Down, Armagh and Londonderry – could be excluded from Home Rule for six years. Asquith followed this up in early 1914 with a proposal that each of the nine Ulster counties, plus the county boroughs of Belfast and Londonderry, could individually vote on whether they also wished to be excluded from the operation of the Third Home Rule Act for the same period. Asquith knew that this would ordinarily mean at least one and perhaps two general elections in the interim, after which any new government could make alternative arrangements. In fact, the Tories had already indicated that if they were elected they would make the exclusion period permanent. Even so, the Liberal proposal prompted an angry reaction from Carson, who said that for Ulster unionists this amounted to a sentence of death with a stay of execution for six years. In addition, the unionists adamantly opposed local plebiscites or referendums, whether on a county basis or any other, as they knew that Home Rule would be accepted not only by Tyrone and Fermanagh with their Catholic majorities but even by Catholic parts of the Protestant heartland such as south Down or north Antrim.

The nationalist response to these latest Liberal proposals was more pragmatic. Faced with growing disillusionment in, and mounting criticism from, Catholic Ireland and in anticipation of getting immediate Home Rule in at least most of Ireland, the nationalist leader John Redmond agreed in February 1914 to accept, temporarily, the exclusion of the six most Protestant counties of Ulster, despite the fact that two of them, Fermanagh and Tyrone, had nationalist majorities. At the same time Bonar Law announced Tory support for the Ulster unionists' preferred option of the permanent exclusion of the same six counties that Redmond was reluctantly prepared to give up temporarily. In effect, therefore, despite further attempted horsetrading at a meeting of party leaders – including Carson and Redmond – at Buckingham Palace in July 1914, this was the state of play on Ireland as the United Kingdom headed for war.

Significantly, at the Buckingham Palace meeting, Carson proposed that the excluded area should have administrative autonomy from the rest of the United Kingdom. This was the first time that unionists had suggested that Ulster should be run in any way differently to the rest of the United Kingdom. When Home Rule became law in September 1914, just after the outbreak of war – although its implementation was postponed for the duration of the conflict – both the Ulster unionists and their Conservative allies had already decided on their preferred option for the border between Ulster and the remainder of Ireland. Neither party deviated from this shared position from that date until the removal of the Irish issue from British politics through the ratification of the six-county border of Northern Ireland at the end of 1925.

When, upon the outbreak of the First World War, Bonar Law proposed national unity and the suspension of normal party politics for the duration of the conflict, Asquith breathed a sigh of relief. In his more optimistic utterances on Ireland, he had stressed his belief that the granting of Home Rule was a concession large enough to keep Ireland quiet and to remove her from the centre of British public life. In his darker moments, he suggested that British policy on Ireland should be to 'submerge the whole lot of them, and their island, for say ten years, under the waves of the Atlantic'.*

Few people in Britain or Ireland at the time would have been prepared to believe that only ten years later Ireland would be divided in two politically, with each part having its own parliament and an international border dividing the island. This was not the inevitable outcome of the political turbulence in Ireland. The most significant factor, however, which determined the establishment of a border, was the constantly changing nature of political developments in both Britain and Ireland over the course of the war and, in particular, the fundamental change in the political balance of power in both countries. In fact, it could be argued that partition and the appearance of an Irish border was the least traumatic of many possible outcomes that could have easily involved bloody civil war and subsequent population transfers – which, ironically, would also have resulted in the same (or a similar) partition and border.

And so, the fact that there would soon be some sort of political border in Ireland was already apparent when war

---

* Michael Laffan, *The Partition of Ireland 1911–1925* (Dundalgan Press, 1983), p 46.

broke out in August 1914. The issues to be resolved were where it was to be, when it would be implemented and whether it would be temporary or permanent. Once the Liberal government had given a commitment that there would be special treatment for Ulster at the conclusion of the war, and once the Conservative opposition and their Ulster unionist allies had agreed that their optimum demand was for the exclusion of six counties, it was only a question of when not if. As the war progressed and the Conservatives as well as the unionist leader Carson entered the wartime coalition Cabinet in May 1915 – followed in December 1916 by the overthrow of Asquith by Lloyd George supported by the Conservatives – it became obvious that the unionist position had strengthened while the nationalist position had weakened. The violence of the republican 1916 Easter Rising only made unionists even more determined to fight for partition: if they were previously unwilling to accept the blandishments of the moderate Home Rulers, they became even more obdurate when faced with the prospect of being ruled by the zealous republican dogmatists who replaced the Home Rulers in nationalist Ireland from 1917 onwards. Redmond and his party recognised that even though Home Rule was now the law of the land, potential power and patronage were rapidly leaching away from them. In desperation, they accepted Lloyd George's post-rising offer of a wartime granting of Home Rule with a temporary exclusion for Carson's six counties. What Redmond failed to realise was that Lloyd George had at the same time indicated to Carson that the exclusion would be permanent. This, in effect, offered the Ulster unionists what they had wanted ever since 1911: the maximum area that they could control.

In the end Lloyd George's machinations were academic, as the southern unionists, whose greatest fear was now isolation in a partitioned Catholic-dominated state rather than Home Rule itself, mobilised their influential Tory allies, particularly those in the House of Lords. They persuasively argued that the granting of Home Rule so soon after the Easter Rising could be interpreted as a reward for treason. Lloyd George's plan thus remained stillborn, but it was significant that this was the first time both nationalists and Ulster unionists had agreed, however fleetingly, on Home Rule with six-county exclusion.

This was followed again in 1917 when, in order to assuage concern in the United States and British Dominions over the British government's Irish policy at this crucial period of the war, Lloyd George once more offered immediate Home Rule with six-county exclusion or, as an alternative, an Irish Convention charged with bringing forward an acceptable scheme of self-government. Lloyd George was particularly anxious about being able to demonstrate to a concerned wider world that the Irish themselves were determining their future rather than being informed what it should be by the imperial parliament. This latest proposal was again scuppered by the Ulster unionists, who were confident that they had already been promised what they wanted: permanent six-county exclusion.

At the end of the war in 1918, Lloyd George – fresh from his victory in the general election but now a Liberal prime minister at the head of a Conservative-dominated peacetime coalition government – had once more to contend with the intractability of Irish politics. As the new government wearily returned to the vexed subject, Liberal Cabinet minister

Winston Churchill, who had supported Home Rule before the war, spoke for the entire Cabinet when he stated that with the Great War 'every institution, almost, in the world was strained'. He went on:

> Great empires have been overturned. The whole map of Europe has been changed… but as the deluge subsides and the waters fall we see the dreary steeples of Fermanagh and Tyrone emerging once again. The integrity of their quarrel is one of the few institutions that have been unaltered in the cataclysm which has swept the world.*

* House of Commons, Hansard, 16 February 1922, vol. 150, col. 1270.

3

The Government of Ireland Act 1920

The 1920 Government of Ireland Act created the new state of Northern Ireland. It is the single most important piece of British legislation of the twentieth century relating to Ireland in that it established a new constitutional and political arrangement (devolved government and partition) which exists to this day. The Act formalised the devolution of government responsibilities to a six-county Northern Ireland that survived the negotiations resulting in the Anglo-Irish Treaty the following year (1921) as well as outlasting the unpublished conclusions of the subsequent Irish Boundary Commission in 1924–5. Although never implemented in the rest of Ireland, the Act also reconfirmed the principle of self-government for the remainder of the island, which was subsequently realised through the Anglo-Irish Treaty with the establishment of the twenty-six county Irish Free State in 1922 and which ultimately became the fully sovereign Republic of Ireland in 1949. Above all, it established the principle of a partitioned Ireland which continues to form the basis of the constitutional arrangement in Ireland today. The Government of Ireland Act was replaced by the Northern Ireland Act 1998 which, subsequent to the Good

Friday Agreement,* re-established a devolved legislature for Northern Ireland following the abolition of the Stormont government in 1972.† The Northern Ireland Act also empowered the British Secretary of State for Northern Ireland to call a referendum or border poll if it appeared likely that a majority of electors in Northern Ireland would prefer to join an all-Ireland state.

Unlike other contenders for the accolade of most significant piece of Anglo-Irish legislation of the last century, the Government of Ireland Act was passed during, not after, a period of intense civil and political strife, involving an escalating guerrilla war by republican separatists against British military and administrative interests in Ireland as well as the spread of rapidly deteriorating intercommunal sectarian strife in the north of the country. In contrast, the 1922 Irish Free State (Agreement) Act gave the force of law to the Anglo-Irish Treaty of the previous year *after* hostilities between Irish republicans and the British state had ceased. Similarly, the Ireland Act of 1949 retrospectively dealt with the constitutional consequences of Ireland's Republic of Ireland Act 1948, such as its exit from the British Commonwealth, as well as reconfirming Northern Ireland's position as part of the United Kingdom. Finally, the Good Friday Agreement and subsequent Northern Ireland Act 1998 followed on from the cessation of a near-thirty-year IRA campaign.

---

* Also known as the Belfast Agreement, the Good Friday Agreement was a peace agreement signed in 1998 to bring an end to the Troubles.
† Stormont, the Northern Ireland parliament, was suspended and direct rule from Westminster reinstated in 1972 because of the deteriorating political and security situation in Northern Ireland.

For such a significant piece of legislation, the 1920 Act is inexplicably overshadowed by preceding proposals that were similar in nature. There were, in effect, four Irish Home Rule Bills dating back to 1886. The earliest fell at the first hurdle in the Commons, the second, in 1893, made it to the Lords but was defeated there and the third made it to the statute book in 1914 but was subsequently overwhelmed by the upheavals of the First World War. All of these proposed varying levels of devolution to a Dublin government, and all of them failed. The fourth Home Rule Bill, which ultimately became the Government of Ireland Act, was the only one even to be partially implemented. Ironically, this implementation only extended to that part of Ireland – the unionist north – that had been most adamant in rejecting Home Rule on the three previous occasions. Meanwhile, the Act's implementation in Home Rule Ireland was a non-starter, with neither nationalist electors nor Irish nationalist politicians being consulted on its proposals.

Although the Government of Ireland Bill was the first Home Rule Bill to propose partition, it was an open secret ever since the passing of the Third Home Rule Act in 1914 that the special provision for Ulster that Prime Minister Asquith constantly referred to would inevitably result in some sort of partition. The British government certainly had contingency plans for such an eventuality as early as 1914. Then, the Chief Secretary for Ireland, Augustine Birrell, had asked three leading Dublin Castle civil servants (his undersecretary Sir James B. Dougherty, W. F. Bailey of the Estates Commissioners' Office and Sir Henry Augustus Robinson, vice-president of the Local Government Board for Ireland) to draw up possible boundaries for an Ulster exclusion zone. Decisions unsympathetic to the wishes of large borderland communities such as Derry and Strabane were made in favour of administrative convenience and were influenced by the strength of militancy amongst both nationalist and unionist extremists in recommending the border of the proposed excluded areas. A classic example was the suggestion by Bailey that both north Cavan and north Monaghan should be in the excluded area, one of the reasons being the militancy of the UVF in these areas. Ultimately, however, the natural conservatism of these civil servants and their desire not to upset the status quo more than necessary led them to propose the continuation of county boundaries as the proposed border: the difficulties created if local government boards, county councils and existing parliamentary constituencies were split across two jurisdictions were obviously too much to contemplate. This line of thinking, which fortuitously coincided with the political outlook of the Ulster unionists and which was carried through to the framing of the Government of Ireland Bill, avoided a fourth partition being proposed by the Bill – not only the partition of the United Kingdom, the partition of Ireland and the partition of Ulster but also the possible partition of individual Ulster counties.

Birrell's civil servants conscientiously produced their recommendations, and copies of their maps were circulated to politicians attending the abortive Buckingham Palace Conference on Ireland in July 1914. As there was no agreement at the conference, and as the country moved towards war and any further negotiation on a settlement in Ireland was postponed for the duration of the conflict, the maps were folded away only to see the light of day when the British government was forced once again to return to the Irish conundrum at the end of the war. By that time, however, the political situation in Ireland, Britain and, indeed, throughout Europe had been overwhelmingly transformed. The republicans were in the ascendant in Ireland, a Conservative-dominated coalition government sympathetic to Ulster unionism ruled in Britain, and in the Europe of the Treaty of Versailles the new watchword was 'self-determination'.

In 1920 the new British government now felt confident and secure enough to offer in peacetime what was impossible to offer in 1916 in wartime: Home Rule for both parts of Ireland, thus satisfying Ulster Unionists. It is important to remember that Ireland was partitioned under the Government of Ireland Act well before hostilities between British forces and the IRA had ceased. This legislation was on the statute book for a year before the Anglo-Irish Treaty, and the Government of Ireland Act's driving principle – partition – was not overturned by it. Partition was facilitated by the newly elected Sinn Féin MPs' abandonment of the House of Commons, which left only a rump of seven Home Rule MPs to argue nationalist Ireland's cause. This vacuum was filled by the only Irish representatives present at Westminster – the Unionists – with their close links to the Conservative Party. Ironically, the nationalist complaint that they were not consulted about the terms of the Government of Ireland Act (because they didn't attend Westminster) was repeated the following year by the unionists, who complained about not being involved in, or at least consulted about, the Anglo-Irish Treaty. From now on the unionists adopted as their guiding star the principles laid down by the Government of Ireland Act from which they refused to be deviated.

In late 1918, after the successful conclusion of the war and following his resounding general election success, Lloyd George had to take immediate action to attempt to resolve the outstanding Irish issue. Legally, the Third Home Rule Act of 1914 was still on the statute book, so some Home Rule in one form or another had to be implemented. The new peacetime coalition government had three options: it could either implement the Home Rule Act with an amending bill to exclude Ulster; it could repeal it; or it could supersede it with new legislation. Lloyd George chose the third option and appointed Walter Long to chair a new Cabinet committee on Ireland which was charged with seeking a way forward. In appointing Long, Lloyd George effectively acknowledged that any new policy must attract widespread Tory as well as unionist support. Long had been Chief Secretary for Ireland in the previous Conservative government and chairman of the Irish Unionist MPs in the House of Commons from 1906 to 1910. His appointment was designed to guarantee the acquiescence of Tory backbenchers and to reassure southern unionists, who still had considerable influence, particularly with Conservative peers, and who were growing increasingly alarmed at the prospect of being abandoned by their fellow unionists in the north. So, by the time Long's committee had begun to meet, Home Rule in its original form was basically dead as a solution to the Irish problem; what's more, in the 1918 general election, the Home Rulers had been replaced in Ireland by more ideological republican separatists, now embarking upon a growing violent insurgency.

The 1920 Government of Ireland Act, which finally established partition, was the ultimate outcome of Long's committee as well as being the direct descendant of the pre-war Third Home Rule Act. Despite the rapid political change that had occurred in both Britain and Ireland since the war, in effect the Act dealt with the Irish political situation as it was before rather than after the war.

In 1918, towards the end of the war, an earlier version of Long's Cabinet committee had, in fact, begun to work within an ideological framework of federalism for the entire British Isles, foreshadowing the basic outlines of what was to become the Government of Ireland Act two years later. Following the Home Rule controversy, this had appeared to many intellectuals to be an attractive proposition that could potentially square the circle of preserving the unity of the United Kingdom while giving political recognition to the diversity inside it. This earlier 1918 committee proposed a Council of Ireland and exclusion for a six-county Ulster, subject to a plebiscite at the end of the war together with a confirmatory referendum seven years later. This early version was rejected by the Cabinet, which believed it was inappropriate to consider such a radical constitutional realignment while the Irish situation was deteriorating so rapidly. In addition, many Conservatives believed that federalism was being used as a convenient device merely to extricate the government from its Irish difficulties. The British Labour Party, however, despite its longstanding official policy of supporting traditional Home Rule, was supportive, and leading members such as J. H. Thomas (who was to become Labour's spokesperson on Ireland) and Arthur Henderson began to suggest the application of the federal principle throughout the United Kingdom. They argued that federalism could be the answer to the dilemma of needing to preserve the union while protecting both Ulster and south-ern Irish unionists and at the same time granting nationalist Ireland what could no longer be denied it. But Ulster union-ists saw federalism as Home Rule by another name – and by 1918 nationalist Ireland had advanced substantially beyond demanding traditional Home Rule as a solution. In the end, Lloyd George felt that it was more important, and more desirable, to deal with the Irish question directly and delay consideration of the larger issue of federalism. Long person-ally believed that the Cabinet had made a mistake in pushing a purely Irish solution rather than a more inclusive federal bill, but Lloyd George's political instincts proved to be correct: federalism was quietly dropped in mid-1918 when it became obvious that it had no mass support in other parts of the United Kingdom, most crucially Scotland and Wales, or in England or amongst Irish nationalists or unionists.

Nevertheless, the controversy over Ireland and the debate as to whether the country's national aspirations could be accommodated within the confines of the United Kingdom as it was constituted at the beginning of the twentieth century did stimulate a lengthy debate on the issue of federalism. It is difficult to appreciate at this remove the extent to which the debate took centre stage during that period. Many con-temporary opinion formers and politicians from all parties believed that a federal reconstituting of the United Kingdom could provide a solution to the seemingly intractable problem of how to reconcile divergent national aspirations in Ireland. They were also convinced that devolution of power to Scotland

and Wales could provide a readjustment of the constitutional equilibrium away from what they interpreted as the unhealthy centralism of power that had been allowed to develop inside the United Kingdom. Even though the arguments for feder-alism were fatally flawed by the fact that the populations of Scotland and Wales evidently did not have the same thirst for Home Rule as the Irish, the influence of the federalist argu-ment can be traced in Lloyd George's proposed solution to the Irish problem as it was in 1919 and 1920. Although the idea of federalism as a solution to the centrifugal forces endangering the integrity of the United Kingdom inevitably declined and collapsed after the decision to allow most of Ireland to leave, it provided the philosophical underpinning for the Govern-ment of Ireland Act of 1920, which would establish Northern Ireland and lay the legislative foundation for the creation of the Irish border the following year.

In October 1919, Long's second Cabinet committee on Ireland agreed to propose separate parliaments for north and south with matters relating to the Crown (defence, foreign affairs, international trade and currency) excluded, alongside a common council with powers for the whole island. In addi-tion, the devolved assemblies were forbidden to make laws aimed at religious discrimination. The theory behind these proposals was that they would ultimately dovetail with the adoption of a federal system of government for the United Kingdom as a whole. Long's proposal was developed into an all-Ireland federal council, the powers of which could be enhanced if the two parliaments together agreed to delegate such authority. This theoretically could satisfy the pledge not to coerce or betray Ulster as well as guaranteeing British withdrawal from all of Ireland. From a British perspective this was an attractive proposition, as it would free Britain from the continuous immersion in Irish problems it had experienced over the previous forty years. The committee rejected calls for a plebiscite, echoing Balfour's criticism that Ireland should not be carved up and treated like a 'conquered' central-European state. Long also betrayed his southern unionist origins when he proposed a nine-county Ulster, as he saw this as ultimately facilitating reunification. The Ulster unionists, however, still committed to what, from their perspective, would be a viable northern political entity, only wanted six counties. The Cabinet, obviously preferring to have the unionists' support for the proposal, consequently backed down; in order to make the whole scheme work, the northern unionists had to be mollified. Despite this concession, all the Ulster Unionist MPs at Westminster voted against the Act. Their preference was for Ulster to remain inside the United Kingdom and so the proposed northern Home Rule state was their default option, although Carson helpfully added that once parliamentary institutions had been granted they could not then be interfered with.

The Government of Ireland Act became law in December 1920. Two parliaments, both bicameral (a House of Lords amendment approved the establishment of a senate in the south in order to bolster southern unionist minorities followed by another amendment proposing one for Northern Ireland), were established. The new six-county state and the Irish border came into existence on 3 May 1921. Lloyd George's main concern, given the Conservative domination of the coalition government, was to provide a solution to the Ulster question that would be congenial to the Tories and their allies, the Ulster unionists, before turning his skills towards negotiating a settlement for the rest of Ireland, where political instability and violence were now endemic. Undoubtedly, the passing of the Government of Ireland Act enabled Lloyd George to satisfy the Ulster unionists and his Conservative government allies prior to commencing negotiations with the resurgent Irish nationalists. As such, the Government of Ireland Act did not coincide with any Irish political aspiration; it was a British coalition Cabinet compromise aimed at delivering the maximum measure of devolution compatible with its own survival and with public, especially Conservative Party, opinion in Britain. In this, as we have seen, Lloyd George was assisted by the refusal of the newly elected Sinn Féin MPs to take their seats at Westminster, which meant that nationalist Ireland had no input into the legislation nor into the parliamentary debate on the subsequent Anglo-Irish Treaty.

From a British perspective, the partition solution establishing two Irish parliaments took Ireland out of the realm of British politics, allowing Britain to withdraw from Ireland on her own terms. Elections for the parliament of Southern Ireland on 24 May 1921 became elections for the republican assembly, the Second Dáil, where Sinn Féin were unopposed in 124 out of 128 seats. The parliament of Southern Ireland met only once (with four unionists), was adjourned *sine die* and was ultimately disbanded by the Irish Free State (Agreement) Act 1922. It ceased to exist on 6 December 1922 when the Irish Free State constitution legally came into existence.

The thinking was that because the Irish could now govern themselves, no Irish person could ever again complain about domination from Westminster. All Ireland was now autonomous, and the eventual reunification of Ireland (a particular concern expressed by Britain's allies the United States and the Dominions) could be facilitated on an agreed basis in accordance with the topical principle of self-determination established recently by the Treaty of Versailles. Even with the benefit of a century of hindsight, it is difficult to imagine an alternative option to partition that would have made sense from the British perspective, if their overriding concern was to withdraw from Ireland without coercing Ulster. If the Home Rulers rather than Sinn Féin had still been the dominant political force in the south, the Government of Ireland Act would have been a brilliant solution. All previous Home Rule had foundered on the rock of unionist opposition. Ironically, the Fourth Home Rule Bill satisfied Ulster (or most of it) but not the extreme nationalists of Sinn Féin, who were the new masters in the south where, as described above, the Government of Ireland Act remained dead amid escalating and relentless political violence. The Act was, however, the only one of the four Home Rule Bills to come into effect, even partially. In this it reflected the new Tory-dominated balance of power at Westminster, but it is an irony that the only part of Ireland not wanting Home Rule was the only part to get it.

From a Conservative perspective it was obvious as early as 1917, if not before, that an Irish settlement involving some sort of Home Rule was essential to the war effort and to bring the Irish-American lobby into the war – and was probably necessary to ensure the survival of the Empire after the war, given the concern and anxiety shown by the Dominions towards Britain's Irish policy. It is also apparent that Conservative support for the Ulster unionist case weakened between 1913 and 1918 – undoubtedly because since 1916 the Conservatives had been the dominant partners in the wartime coalition government and so no longer needed to 'play the Orange card', that is, to align with unionists in Ireland for political gain in the quest for office. Furthermore, as the Irish crisis intensified it became increasingly obvious to both parties that although their short-term interests might coincide, the Conservatives were ultimately concerned about the future post-war welfare of the United Kingdom as a whole, whereas the Ulster unionists' overriding concern was for their own identity in Ireland.

Labour Party attitudes to Ireland were also changing. Prior to and even after the war, the Labour Party had provided general, vague and unthinking support for the political demands of moderate Irish nationalism. It became clear, however, that if the Labour Party aspired to become the governing party in the British state, it had to distance itself from the revolutionary politics that had rapidly come to dominate Irish nationalism since 1918. Unlike the Conservatives, the Labour Party had no political debts to pay in Ireland. There had never been a cohesive and logically planned Irish policy in the Labour Party. For historical reasons nearly all the party (except in Belfast) had a deep and genuinely held emotional attachment to the moderate policies of the Home Rulers. Labour shared the Home Rulers' abhorrence of partition as a threat to the territorial integrity of Ireland. Consequently, Labour opposition to the Government of Ireland Act provided certainty to its supporters and voters at a time when its own policies on Ireland were in a state of flux, as it was increasingly criticised for slavishly following the traditional Home Rule policy when it was obvious that mainstream political demands in nationalist Ireland had moved well beyond that. Inevitably the party's cautious constitutionalism and parliamentarianism began to be threatened by its more radical members and some (although not a majority) of its Irish voters in Britain, who demanded direct action and a closer identification with the extra-parliamentary nationalism of Sinn Féin.

The Irish border demarcating the six counties of Northern Ireland from the rest of the country became a reality on 3 May 1921. Ironically, it first of all separated a Home Rule Northern Ireland from the bulk of the island that was still run directly from Westminster. Initially, Ulster unionists had been suspicious of the offer of a separate parliament in Belfast, fearing that it was some sort of dastardly ploy to detach them from the rest of the United Kingdom by treating them as semi-detached members who at some stage in the future could be delivered into the jaws of an all-Ireland state. They quickly warmed to the idea, however, when they saw that a separate parliament for Ulster, permanently controlled by unionists and in charge of their own security, gave them added insurance against peremptory expulsion from the United Kingdom in the future. From then on, all the political energies of the unionists would be directed into maintaining the border that had come into existence that spring.

4

The Anglo-Irish Treaty

On 22 June 1921, only six weeks after the establishment of Northern Ireland, George V opened the new parliament in Belfast. The king was apprehensive at what he perceived to be the triumphalist nature of the proposed speech he was expected to deliver, written for him by Ulster Unionists including Sir James Craig. He expressed his concern to Jan Smuts and others, who crafted a more emollient speech in which the king pleaded for forbearance and conciliation and thus provided the right atmosphere for a peace initiative and an end to the escalating guerrilla warfare between the Crown and republican forces throughout Ireland.

Whether or not the king was instrumental in initiating the subsequent events that led to a truce being called the following month and which resulted ultimately in the Anglo-Irish Treaty at the end of the year, it was certainly in both Britain's and Ireland's interests that hostilities should cease. From a British perspective, the fact that Ulster was now secure enabled the government to consider entering negotiations with Sinn Féin to agree a political solution for the rest of the island. Lloyd George was by now acutely aware of the unpopularity and growing unacceptability in Britain of the continuing

Irish War of Independence. Furthermore, the official policy of reprisals and counter-terror was damaging Britain's international reputation. In Britain deep revulsion and outrage was articulated most effectively by church leaders, trade unionists, newspapers and opposition politicians. For Lloyd George it was obvious that he now had only two options in Ireland: all-out war and military rule or a truce and subsequent negotiations. This, allied to the prime minister's realisation that Irish nationalist demands for self-determination now far outstripped the original modest demand for Home Rule and that Sinn Féin did articulate the wishes of a majority of Irish nationalists, propelled the government towards a truce. It was also apparent that the Government of Ireland Act of the previous year was now defunct in the south with the result that a political and constitutional vacuum was now looming in most of Ireland. How was it now to be governed, given that Sinn Féin had resolutely rejected the concept of a Home Rule parliament in southern Ireland complementing that of the newly created Northern Ireland?

At the same time, Sinn Féin and the IRA were facing a potential political and military crisis. The capture of men and weapons and the effects of war weariness meant, as IRA leader Michael Collins later admitted, that the republican guerrilla campaign could only have survived for another three weeks from the date of the truce in July 1921. Collins also realised (more than some of his comrades) that the logic of an underground army emerging from the shadows meant that a political agreement, no matter how unpalatable to some, was inevitable. A military truce, the longer it continued, would not only enervate the cutting edge the IRA provided to the republican campaign but, once out in the open, it was almost impossible to ever again recover the mystique and effectiveness of a previously subterranean guerrilla struggle. Consequently, it was in both sides' interests to call a halt to military action and instead seek a political solution to the crisis.

Both the progress of the Government of Ireland Bill (October 1919 to December 1920) and the negotiations that led from the truce to the Anglo-Irish Treaty (July to December 1921) took place amid a level of political violence not seen in Ireland for well over a century. Ironically, very little of this violence took place in the area most affected by partition – the proposed border area. The first IRA attacks took place in early 1919, and for much of that year the violence was relatively sporadic and low key. The IRA then started to attack Royal Irish Constabulary (RIC) patrols and barracks, forcing isolated barracks to be abandoned. British troops were originally regarded as acting in support of the civil authority – that is, the police – but early in 1920 the British government established two paramilitary police units – the Black and Tans and the Auxiliaries – to support the police as well. Both these organisations' reputations for ill discipline and reprisals, allied to the introduction of martial law, led to the escalation of violence in late 1920 as the IRA campaign became more organised and militant until the truce in July 1921.

The IRA's campaign was mainly, although not exclusively, a southern affair. Despite the rhetoric and drilling at the time of the Ulster Crisis between 1912 and 1914, violence did not come to Ulster until the summer of 1920. One of the main reasons for this comparative calm was the continued influence of constitutional nationalism amongst the Catholic population, particularly in Belfast and Derry. The new Sinn Féin philosophy was largely southern; it was also distinctly rural – though it failed to make much ground even in the more rural parts of Ulster. Belfast Catholics had been the least militant of the nationalist population, as was evidenced by their enthusiastic commitment to the British war effort particularly during the opening years of the First World War. In the 1918 general election, the Home Rulers managed to fight off the Sinn Féin assault by returning four of its remaining six MPs from what was shortly to become Northern Ireland. Irish Home Rulers in the north instinctively knew that a campaign of violent confrontation would invariably lead to an increase in sectarianism in which northern Catholics would suffer the most. Furthermore, such violence would only embolden rather than weaken Ulster unionist obduracy and control of the province. In contrast to the rest of Ireland, where the lack of any meaningful political opposition had resulted in the Home Rulers becoming complacent, in the north there was a unionist opposition that required a permanent grassroots nationalist political machine ready to fight for every last vote. A potent political mixture of the charismatic leader Joe Devlin, the Catholic Church, and the Catholic lay organisation the Ancient Order of Hibernians, saw off Sinn Féin pretty effectively with Devlin easily beating Sinn Féin president Éamon de Valera for the nationalist seat of West Belfast. Consequently, the IRA campaign in the north was largely confined to rural Catholic areas and even there support remained modest as a result of the danger of provoking retaliatory sectarian attacks on the Catholic population.

All of this began to change in the summer of 1920. Earlier

in the year, as the IRA campaign in the south and west gained traction, the incipient Northern Ireland remained largely peaceful. But then, over a seven-day period in June, in Derry twenty people were shot in gun battles between the UVF and IRA. This was followed by the expulsion of Catholic workers from the Belfast shipyards and ancillary industries following the return to work after the 12 July holidays. The violence extended to streets around the shipyards and led to four days of rioting in which it is estimated that eight thousand Catholic and left-leaning Protestant workers were expelled from their jobs. The immediate catalyst for all this had been the murder of a senior northern RIC officer in Cork, but underlying tensions, such as the competition for jobs, also complicated the situation. None of the expelled shipyard workers would ever return to work, and this exacerbated the already high levels of poverty and unemployment amongst the Catholic population in Belfast. The heightened tension was increased by the prospect of extended political uncertainty as a result of the imminence of partition. Although roughly coinciding with the Anglo-Irish War, or the Irish War of Independence, the sectarian conflict in Belfast between 1920 and 1922 was unique in its characteristics. Unlike the rest of Ireland, which saw essentially a guerrilla war between the IRA and Crown forces, 90 per cent of the deaths in Belfast and its environs were civilian, either as a result of sectarian assassinations or armed conflict between the two communities. Ironically, paramilitary organisations such as the IRA and UVF seemed to be following rather than leading a spontaneous communal conflict. Furious loyalist mobs destroyed over three hundred Catholic homes, businesses and religious buildings in Lisburn,

Co. Antrim in August 1920 following the IRA assassination of an RIC district inspector in the town. As a result, over a thousand Catholics fled to Newry, Dundalk and Belfast, joining the Catholic refugees from the civil disturbance in the east Belfast shipyards the previous month.

This was the culmination of six weeks of violence in Belfast and nearby towns as nationalist victories under the new proportional representation system in local elections, including Derry, unnerved many Protestants in the run-up to partition and led directly to the establishment of the Ulster Special Constabulary.* It was apparent in the summer of 1920 that the existing UVF could not control loyalist outrages so, in July, Winston Churchill, the police chief – Lieutenant-General Sir Henry Tudor – and Craig proposed to Lloyd George that the formation of a special constabulary could potentially free up police and military resources in the north. However, loyalists in Lisburn and Lisnaskea – along with Sir Basil Brooke, later premier of Northern Ireland, at Colebrooke in Fermanagh – had already established unofficial constabularies, all of which were opposed by Sir John Anderson, joint under-secretary at Dublin Castle, as he considered them likely to provoke sectarian violence. Craig then proposed to Lloyd George a two-thousand-strong special constabulary in September 1920. There were reservations from army chief General Nevil Macready, who feared civil war, and from Sir Henry Wilson who wanted the USC, and primarily the B-Specials, under military control – but basically

---

* The Ulster Special Constabulary, which included the B-Specials, was a loyalist reserve police force.

Craig could now arm unionists aged between twenty-one and forty-five (later extended to the entire male unionist population) so that he had not only the Special Constabulary but also the UVF in reserve – all of this six months before Northern Ireland came into being. The initial fear amongst the unionist population was that these reservists could be sent anywhere in Ireland, but, once it became obvious that they could only serve in their own districts, recruitment began to pick up. Violence in Belfast peaked again between April and June 1921, a period of intense militant activity by the IRA in the south but also the time Northern Ireland came into existence and its parliament was opened. There was another spike in November and December 1921, during the Treaty negotiations in London and the transfer of security powers to the new Northern Ireland government. And in the spring and summer of 1922 renewed tensions led to civil disturbance as the two new Irish states confronted each other for the first time. Belfast accounted for 40 per cent of all fatalities in Ireland during this period, with five hundred people killed between July 1920 and June 1922 and twenty thousand forced to move as refugees or expelled from their places of work. Belfast Catholics accounted for two-thirds of the casualties and the vast majority of refugees and workplace expulsions. The violence of this period produced more casualties than all the riots of the previous century put together. Such was the level of paranoia amongst unionists that isolated shootings on the border became attempted invasions by the time the news reached Belfast. Ironically, it was exactly this level of violence that partition was supposed to prevent. It wasn't until June 1922 with the outbreak of civil war in the south that political attention was removed from Belfast and it returned to relative normality.

By the summer of 1921 it was obvious both to the British and to Irish republicans that attempts should be made to fit the final piece into the jigsaw of Anglo-Irish relations – the future relationship between nationalist Ireland and the British Empire. In the same way as the British government sought to secure its rear by resolving the Ulster question through the Government of Ireland Act – thus removing most if not all of any Conservative reservations there may have been over the whole issue of the threat to coerce Ulster – before tackling the conundrum that was the rest of Ireland, so Sinn Féin and the IRA sought to maximise their advantage through military means in the south of Ireland before agreeing to talk to the British.

Irish republicans seemed to have little idea as to what their policy on the north should be. The new republican assembly, Dáil Éireann, rarely discussed the situation there and, when it did, it invariably showed its lack of awareness and ignorance of the subtleties of life in the northern province. In 1920, in response to attacks on Catholics in the north, Sinn Féin introduced an embargo on all goods and services from the Protestant north-east. This Belfast boycott was intended to emphasise Ulster's dependence on the rest of the country as well as reinstating expelled Catholic dock workers in their jobs. Heavy industry such as shipbuilding and engineering had little business with the south and so remained immune, but banking and other services were severely damaged. Little was achieved in the long term, and the boycott also negatively affected northern Catholics, who were meant to be the main beneficiaries of the policy, as well as provoking similar boy-cotts against Protestant businesses in the south. The net effect was to reinforce a sense of psychological partition – that the two parts of Ireland had little in common with each other – which anticipated the decision of the new Irish state to introduce a customs border between north and south in 1923.

The July 1921 truce initiated a convoluted series of discussions between London and Dublin that meandered on until October when meaningful negotiations began. During the preliminaries, Lloyd George offered de Valera Dominion status like Canada or Australia but rejected any unravelling of the Government of Ireland Act which had set up Northern Ireland the previous year. By the time formal negotiations commenced in October 1921, Northern Ireland had already been established with a functioning parliament and government. Departmental responsibilities and a security service were in the process of being established in the north while the Treaty negotiations were taking place. In effect, a unionist state was already a reality.

When the negotiations started, the Irish delegation concentrated on the future constitutional relationship between Ireland and Britain; whether the new Ireland should remain in the Empire and whether an oath of fidelity should be given to the British monarch as head of the Empire. These were largely symbolic topics that avoided the emotive issue of partition. The Irish argument was for the British to stand aside and allow Irishmen to resolve their differences, whereas the British promoted themselves as being motivated by no more than benevolent neutrality – though they were adamant that the Government of Ireland Act had already established Northern

Ireland and that, as a result, Ulster could not be coerced into an unacceptable constitutional arrangement. Lloyd George was acutely conscious, however, that continuing to refuse to allow a plebiscite in Northern Ireland ran counter to the Treaty of Versailles and the current fashion for self-determination. The plebiscite to determine the disputed Silesian frontier between a defeated Germany and the new Poland occupied much of the news during 1921, and Lloyd George knew that he could expect to be attacked on this front by the Irish delegation at some stage during the negotiations. The problem for Lloyd George was that the outcome of any county plebiscite in Northern Ireland would inevitably transfer Tyrone and Fermanagh out of Northern Ireland thus undermining the Government of Ireland settlement of the previous year.

The negotiations that led to the Anglo-Irish Treaty continued in a desultory manner for two months, concluding in December 1921. From time to time Ulster would occupy centre stage, but most of the discussion was on the constitutional relationship of Ireland to the Crown and the wider British Empire. Once it became apparent in November that the unionists remained obdurate, refusing even to consider an all-Ireland parliament or a reduction in the size of the northern state, Lloyd George offered the Irish delegation the prospect of a Boundary Commission to determine the nature of the border between the two Irelands. Even at this stage, the Irish realised that such an offer could, at the very most, transfer nationalist areas to the south but would never result in the implosion of Northern Ireland and the unity of the whole island. Nevertheless, the Sinn Féin delegation and Arthur Griffith in particular agreed not to oppose Lloyd

George on the Boundary Commission proposal as Lloyd George attempted to browbeat the unionists with the threat of a Boundary Commission coming into operation. He also pointed out to the unionists that the future tax burden for Northern Ireland would be far more onerous if it remained part of the United Kingdom rather than becoming part of an all-Ireland Dominion.

Northern Ireland's response was even more stubborn, with James Craig demanding Dominion status for Northern Ireland separate from the rest of Ireland. This was probably the most difficult time for the Ulster unionists during these negotiations, as their audacious demand alienated many of their previous supporters in Britain and caused anxiety amongst their Conservative allies, who realised that public opinion in Britain was not as sympathetic to the plight of the embattled unionists as it had been a decade earlier during the Ulster Crisis of 1912–14. However, the unionists held their nerve; the proposal for some sort of all-Ireland assembly, which was preferred by both the British and Irish negotiators, was dropped and debate moved towards the Boundary Commission proposal, which all sides knew could, at the very most, involve some sort of readjustment of the border.

A Boundary Commission was first formally proposed at negotiations in mid-November when the British suggested that if the northern parliament refused to participate in an all-Ireland parliament, then a Commission would be established to determine the boundary between the two parts of Ireland. What was to become Article 12 of the Anglo-Irish Treaty stated quite clearly that a Boundary Commission 'shall determine in accordance with the wishes of the inhabitants, so far as may be compatible with economic and geographic conditions the boundaries between Northern Ireland and the rest of Ireland'. The Irish managed to alter the conditions so that each government could appoint a commissioner rather than the British appointing all members, but they failed to challenge the phrase 'economic and geographic conditions' in the article, which was to have serious implications for the amendment of the boundary when the Commission met in 1924–5. Furthermore, the Irish negotiators failed to demand specific information as to whether the Commission would have the ability to make recommendations all the way from small-scale land transfers to making even the idea of Northern Ireland unviable. It's as if Sinn Féin believed that, in some mercurial and unspecified way, the Commission would 'deliver' for the south. After all, the Anglo-Irish Treaty theoretically postulated one government for the whole island even though Northern Ireland was given the opportunity of opting out.

When the draft Treaty was discussed in Dublin, de Valera had rejected the right of any part of Ireland to opt out of the new Irish state. Nationalist Ireland was prepared to allow Northern Ireland to retain its own territory (except for local plebiscites to determine the exact nature of the contested border), parliament and government as long as these were subordinate to Dublin rather than to London. This became known during Treaty negotiations as 'essential unity' – a phrase coined by Arthur Griffith – but, overall, the discussion on Ulster was overshadowed by other issues, such as the proposed oath of fidelity to the king, with the result that when the Irish proposed amendments to the British draft Treaty none of them included any reference to Ulster. The British accepted some of these amendments, and on the evening of 6 December 1921 the Irish signed the Treaty. When the Treaty was debated in Dublin, the Cabinet was split, and Dáil Éireann entered into rancorous debate on the old symbolic issues of the Crown, the Empire and the oath – with Northern Ireland and the Boundary Commission hardly featuring. It is somewhat symbolic that the future of Northern Ireland occupied only nine out of 338 paragraphs of the record of the Treaty debates in December 1921 and January 1922.

Ironically, both pro- and anti-Treaty elements in Dáil Éireann supported the Boundary Commission proposal, as it seemed to promise the end or, at least, a dilution, of partition. This is despite the fact that the major issue affecting partition in the Anglo-Irish Treaty was the Boundary Commission proposal. But partition itself at this stage was an abstract concept and really only became a practical issue with the establishment of a new, independent nationalist government in the south the following year. Even though the Irish negotiators knew how anxious the unionists were about the uncertainty created by this proposal, they failed to examine the issue forensically. What exactly the British meant by 'economic and geographic conditions' was never probed, and so the scene was set for the Irish Boundary Commission to determine where the border between north and south should lie. The Commission's recommendations – or, more specifically, the response of the three governments to these recommendations – determined the nature of the boundary for the next century.

Signed on 6 December 1921, the Articles of Agreement for a Treaty Between Great Britain and Ireland – as the Anglo-Irish Treaty was officially known – created the Irish Free State with Dominion status similar to that pertaining at the time in Canada and Australia. In fact, Article 2 of the Treaty specified that the relationship of the Crown and the imperial parliament to the new Dominion should be that of the United Kingdom and the Dominion of Canada. The new political entity would take on a share of the United Kingdom national debt and would not raise a defence force greater, in proportion to the population, than that of the United Kingdom. British use of three ports – the so-called Treaty Ports – in peacetime and other facilities in war were guaranteed, but after five years Irish defence of the coast was conceded, subject to agreement by joint conference. The provisions in respect of Northern Ireland maintained the terms of the 1920 Government of Ireland Act for a month after the official establishment of the Irish Free State (this took place when the Irish Free State Constitution Act received royal assent on 5 December 1922) during which Northern Ireland could opt out of the new settlement. If this happened, the status quo of Northern Ireland staying in the United Kingdom would remain. If Ulster chose to join the Free State, the Northern Ireland parliament would remain but as a devolved assembly from Dublin. But if Northern Ireland opted out of the Free State, Article 12 of the Treaty provided for the establishment of a Boundary Commission with three representatives – one from Northern Ireland, one from the Free State and one from the United Kingdom – in order to determine the boundary 'in accordance with the wishes of the inhabitants so far as may be compatible with economic and geographic conditions'. On 7 December 1922, Northern Ireland exercised its right under the Treaty to remain outside the Irish Free State.

The Treaty offered Irish nationalists complete independence in domestic affairs (including full fiscal autonomy) in the 26-county jurisdiction. It is also arguable that, given the rapidly evolving nature of Dominion status inside the British Commonwealth, its 'external' freedoms would be wide ranging and likely to expand. The Irish negotiators were persuaded by Lloyd George to accept the Treaty because he argued that Ireland's 'essential unity' was given recognition, first of all by the facility of allowing Northern Ireland to join the Irish Free State if it chose to and, if it didn't, by the continuation of the Council of Ireland* from the 1920 Act. In addition, the Irish Boundary Commission could potentially redraw the border, and there was an expectation (or hope) on the republican side, which Lloyd George assiduously cultivated, that the transfer of much of the territory occupied by the substantial Roman Catholic community in Northern Ireland to the Irish Free State would make it difficult for the northern state to survive. It was a substantial negotiating achievement on the part of Lloyd George to give the impression to the Irish representatives that the establishment of a Boundary Commission would lead to Irish unity, especially as he had maintained throughout negotiations that the British government was rigidly adhering to the two conditions that Ireland must remain part of the Empire and that Ulster must not be coerced. Despite this, the Irish signed, convinced that the Commission was their best chance to end partition.

As regards British domestic politics, Ireland began to fade

---

* The all-Ireland forum proposed by the Government of Ireland Act to discuss issues of interest or concern to both Irish jurisdictions.

into the background in the years after the First World War. It had been a divisive issue in British politics both before and during the war and, indeed, had dominated party politics in the House of Commons on and off since 1886; now, after the upheaval of the war, it assumed the appearance of a wearisome irritation. It was still likely to rear up and disrupt the predictability of British party politics, but it was a problem that had remained unresolved for years and so really needed to be solved permanently. There was now a new political spirit in post-war Britain as all parties began to become more involved with social and economic concerns and began to move away from fixation with the rights and wrongs of the competing nationalisms in Ireland. Although there had been popular support for Ulster unionists in Britain before the war, that support did not survive in the post-war years except amongst the right wing of the Conservative Party. There was no permanent constituency in Britain ready to defend Ulster's interests equivalent to the Irish-American lobby in support of nationalist Ireland. Ulster unionists began to be perceived, even amongst their erstwhile supporters, as obdurate and stubborn, unwilling to compromise in the interests of the greater good and constantly demanding more financial support from the British exchequer.

In Britain, politics moved on; in Ireland, they stayed the same. There developed a new sense of British identity, which increasingly revolved around Anglocentrism and an anxiety to adapt the Empire into a Commonwealth as befitted the rapidly changing political and social landscape of the interwar years. The Irish conundrum was increasingly considered an obsolescent issue in British politics, albeit one with

continued potential to cause political embarrassment and turbulence. As a result of changing circumstances, first the Ulster
unionists in 1920 and then the Irish republicans in 1921 were
manoeuvred into positions where compromise was deemed
to be more acceptable than outright victory. This was made
possible by a combination of coalition politics in immediate
post-war Britain plus a major shift in British public opinion
that demanded that Ireland finally be placed outside the realm
of British party politics.

The continuation of the wartime coalition arrangement
into peacetime British politics undoubtedly facilitated the
government's attempts to solve the Irish problem in 1920–21.
As we have seen, it enabled Lloyd George, the Liberal prime
minister at the head of a government in which the Conservatives were by far the largest contingent, to move first to satisfy
Ulster unionist anxieties by establishing Northern Ireland and
an Irish border through the Government of Ireland Act in
1920. This provided Ulster unionists with the guarantee they
had sought ever since the Ulster Crisis of 1912–14 that they
would not be absorbed against their will into an all-Ireland
system of government.

It was only after Ulster (and the Conservative Party) was
reassured by the Government of Ireland Act that Lloyd
George was able to deal with militant republicans in the
south. The southern negotiators, led by Michael Collins, were
adamant that the Anglo-Irish Treaty should supersede the
previous year's Government of Ireland Act in the same way
as that Act had replaced the pre-war Home Rule legislation;
but Ulster unionists were adamant that this was not their
understanding: the Anglo-Irish Treaty, with its introduction

of a Boundary Commission that could potentially amend the border, threatened the viability of Northern Ireland in a way that the Government of Ireland Act did not. 'What we have we hold,' was the repeated refrain of Northern Ireland's prime minister, the unionist Sir James Craig, asserting the unionists' commitment to the Government of Ireland Act. The Act had not only established the panoply of a separate legislature in Northern Ireland but also established a border which, to the unionists, was now inviolate. In their eyes, it was not the Anglo-Irish Treaty that had created partition; it had already been created the year before by the Government of Ireland Act.

The further irony was that the Anglo-Irish Treaty was supposed to facilitate the future unification of Ireland, creating as it did one government for the Irish Free State, a Dominion of the British Commonwealth (which included the six previously excluded counties). In reality, as we have seen, it temporarily suspended the new government's jurisdiction over Northern Ireland and allowed the Ulster parliament to permanently exclude itself from the new Irish Free State – a choice that it took immediately. After this permanent self-exclusion, the terms of the 1920 Act remained in force. These terms included more restrictive financial provisions for Northern Ireland than it would have enjoyed as part of the Irish Free State, which had been granted fiscal independence by the Treaty, so there had been a very real financial inducement for the unionists to join a united Ireland. Furthermore, Northern Ireland's decision to exclude itself from the Irish Free State triggered the establishment of a Boundary Commission to determine the permanent course of the Irish border.

The presence of Conservative ministers – upholders of Ulster unionist interests – in Lloyd George's coalition government and as signatories of the Anglo-Irish Treaty was meant to enable Ireland to be defused, finally, as a potent issue in British politics. The Conservatives were in a strategic position to ensure that Lloyd George had to take into account unionist fears and susceptibilities when negotiating with the representatives of radical Irish nationalism. The Conservative leadership was also, by and large, able to keep its die-hard pro-unionist element in check and to stop it sabotaging any potential accommodation to be arrived at between the government and Sinn Féin.

Notwithstanding this, the provision for a Boundary Commission in the Anglo-Irish Treaty caused immediate consternation amongst all unionists and many Conservatives. The Treaty did not specify whether the Commission would have the ability to make only minor adjustments to the new border or whether it would be able to transfer sufficient swathes of Northern Ireland to the new Free State in a way that could render partition unviable and reunification inevitable. The central issue of the Anglo-Irish Treaty – the future relationship of nationalist Ireland to the United Kingdom – was thus replaced by a new controversy over the future of the Irish border, despite the fact that the very existence of the Boundary Commission clause in the Treaty was a tacit acceptance of the fact that a separate and already established Northern Ireland would be able to exercise its right to opt out of a united Ireland. In reality, the Boundary Commission proposal posed no real threat to the Ulster unionists, despite the consternation it caused. It was understandable that that element should cause such (ultimately misplaced) anxiety to unionists, but the furore it led to overshadowed the fact that in the negotiations nationalist Ireland had been presented with a fait accompli.

With Northern Ireland already in possession of a functioning parliament, government and security apparatus, the constitutional position of Protestant Ulster had already been secured by the time the fate of the rest of the country was decided. During the Treaty negotiations, the representatives of the doctrinaire republicans of Sinn Féin considered the principle of independence from Westminster and total Irish sovereignty to be more important than the supposedly temporary exclusion of the six north-eastern counties. But this position would ultimately lead to the Irish Civil War after the Treaty had been agreed.

5

The Politics of the Irish Boundary Commission

The Anglo-Irish Treaty of December 1921, which effectively gave Dominion Home Rule to a partitioned Ireland, under-pinned the principles of the Government of Ireland Act of the previous year, albeit with enhanced independence for the proposed Irish Free State. For both Conservatives and Liberals in the coalition government, the Treaty, on closer inspection, seemed to be at odds with both parties' traditional stances on Ireland: one defending the unity of the United Kingdom and the other prepared to advance limited self-government to the island as a whole. However, there was not much in the way of 'closer inspection'; for both coalition parties (and indeed for the country as a whole) the Treaty was a pragmatic solution to the age-old intractable problem of Ireland given that Lloyd George had now 'conjured it out of existence'.*

On 7 January 1922, the Treaty was approved by Dáil Éireann by the perilously close margin of sixty-four to fifty-seven votes. Opposition came from the die-hard republicans out of step with popular sentiment in the south. In the imme-diate aftermath of the narrow acceptance of the Treaty, both

---

* A.J.P. Taylor, *English History: 1914–1945* (Clarendon Press, 1965) p 236.

pro- and anti-Treaty elements in the IRA manoeuvred to get their forces into the key military positions vacated by British forces in the opening months of 1922. Meanwhile, the Provisional Government, established under the Treaty, appeared reluctant to confront its anti-Treaty former comrades-in-arms. Throughout the spring of 1922, the situation in Ireland deteriorated rapidly, and on 15 April the Four Courts in Dublin were occupied by anti-Treaty forces. The following month, in a desperate attempt to prevent the outbreak of violence between former comrades, the two sides of Sinn Féin agreed a coalition pact for the first general election in the putative Free State. This was an attempt by the Provisional Government to avoid both a total rupture with the anti-Treaty elements and a possible civil war, proposing a national Sinn Féin ticket in proportion to the existing strength of the pro- and anti-Treaty forces in Dáil Éireann. These manoeuvrings were viewed with apprehension by the British government as being in breach of the Treaty, but the election went ahead anyway and resulted in a large majority for the pro-Treaty element in Sinn Féin. However, it was obvious that the south was moving inexorably towards civil war, and one of the significant consequences of this was that Sir James Craig and the northern government refused to have any further dealings with the Provisional Government or with the proposed Boundary Commission. The situation worsened when, on 22 June 1922, Sir Henry Wilson – a consistent and ardent anti-republican who was recently elected as a Unionist MP for North Down and was the security advisor to the Northern Ireland government and former chief of the Imperial General Staff – was assassinated in London. The British government naturally assumed that this was the responsibility of the anti-Treaty republican forces and instructed the Provisional Government in the south to take action against the occupiers of the Four Courts. With that, the Irish Civil War started. As the summer progressed and the fratricidal civil conflict in Ireland quickened, Lloyd George's coalition government finally fell in October and was replaced by a totally Conservative administration under Bonar Law.

The election of the new Conservative administration – especially one led by Bonar Law given his past unionist sympathies – created some doubt initially as to whether the legislation required for the ratification of the Irish Free State would be passed. The Irish Free State (Agreement) Act had approved the Anglo-Irish Treaty, but the Irish Free State (Constitution) Bill had to be passed before the new state could officially come into being. However, Bonar Law obviously demurred at the prospect of allowing Ireland to continue dominating British politics and, despite his personal reservations as well as those of his backbenchers, introduced the Bill into the Commons in November. It was passed the following month, and the Irish Free State finally came into legal existence on 6 December 1922.

But Bonar Law resigned as Conservative prime minister in May 1923 and died six months later. He was replaced by Stanley Baldwin, whose sudden commitment to protectionism rather than free trade as a basic tenet of Conservative Party policy led directly to the December 1923 general election. Called when the government still commanded a massive majority and with four years of its tenure left to run, the election propelled a minority Labour administration into office for the first time ever in January 1924.

Prominent Tories such as Bonar Law and Stanley Baldwin

were relieved that the coalition government had produced the Treaty, as it meant that there was no going back to the uncertainty of the immediate post-war years. However, they kept these sentiments quiet at the time, fearing that they might be associated with the alleged betrayal of Ulster. Despite Conservative unease with the terms of the Treaty and particularly the provision for a Boundary Commission, leading Tories, including Bonar Law and Baldwin, judged that the time was finally right for Ireland to be removed from British politics. However, the central issue of Anglo-Irish relations, namely the status of Ulster and the future of the Irish border, refused to disappear. The problem in 1924, as the Irish Boundary Commission controversy began to escalate, remained the same as it had been in 1921 or 1914: because a decision on the future of Northern Ireland had merely been postponed by the Anglo-Irish Treaty and not settled, it returned to haunt British politics. The unresolved Irish issue contributed to the end of Lloyd George's career, as the Tories increasingly regarded him as erratic, corrupt and untrustworthy. The new Tory prime minister, Stanley Baldwin, regarded Lloyd George as a 'dynamic force'* who had destroyed his own party, the Liberals, and whose greatest achievement – the Anglo-Irish Treaty and, in particular, the unpredictable issue of the Boundary Commission – was likely to return the volatile Irish issue to the forefront of British politics unless dealt with.

The Treaty finally ended Britain's direct involvement in Irish political affairs both north and south, but the interpretation of

---

* This phrase was used at a Carlton Club meeting of Conservative MPs on 19 October 1922.

what exactly the Treaty meant was to bedevil relations, not only inside the Irish Free State – where it led directly to a civil war far more vicious than the guerrilla campaign against the British – but between the two parts of Ireland and between both Irish states and successive British governments. The most immediate source of dispute was the vexed issue of Article 12 of the Treaty regarding a Boundary Commission. Much of the time of the first Labour government in 1924 was spent attempting to resolve the final remaining imponderable of the Anglo-Irish Treaty, namely deciding on the boundary between the newly established Irish Free State and the six counties of Northern Ireland as established under the Government of Ireland Act of 1920.

The Northern Ireland prime minister, Sir James Craig, was extremely wary in his initial dealings with the new Labour government. This was because the unionists believed that an incoming Labour administration would be overly sympathetic to the aims and ideals of Irish nationalists and, in particular, the nationalist position on the forthcoming Boundary Commission. However, in their contribution to the House of Commons debate on the Treaty, Labour MPs had made no reference to the boundary controversy; indeed, anti-partitionism was the one issue that united the entire spectrum of Labour opinion on Ireland. Furthermore, in supporting the Treaty and, by implication, Article 12, they at least tacitly accepted partition, albeit with the possibility of a revision of the boundary. This, however, was not the interpretation of the Ulster unionists. For them, the Irish Boundary Commission was a sword of Damocles hanging over their heads. Potentially, it was a device that could consign them to the less than tender mercies of an all-Ireland state. It was also something that was imposed upon them without their consent by the forces of Irish nationalism and by Lloyd George's coalition government in London desperate to extricate itself from the morass of Irish politics and its debilitating effect on British political life. Unionist suspicion and anxiety were fuelled by the resignation and subsequent death in 1923 of their traditional protector in the Conservative Party, Bonar Law, and they were paranoid about the possibility of any further British government formed by either the Asquithian Liberals (following the split in 1916 from Lloyd George's disciples) or the Labour Party. In fact, this anxiety was one of the main reasons why, in 1920, the Ulster Unionists wanted their own parliament: it was to be a bulwark against a hostile British government at Westminster.

The Unionists retained this suspicious attitude towards the new Labour government because of its historical sympathy for Irish nationalism. Furthermore, Unionists believed that the Northern Ireland boundary had already been legally established by the Government of Ireland Act of 1920 rather than by the Anglo-Irish Treaty of 1921. The spectre of the Boundary Commission was still creating such anxiety in 1924 because its establishment was substantially delayed as a result of a number of political factors developing in Ireland after 1921. First was the chaos of the civil war and the insecurity of the new Free State government. Then there was the determined non-cooperation of the government of Northern Ireland, reinforced by the Collins–de Valera electoral pact* of

---

* This pact sought to avoid a split in Sinn Féin by agreeing that a national coalition panel of candidates representing both pro- and anti-Treaty wings would stand in the 1922 Free State general election.

May 1922. Craig was also adamant that he would not countenance any Boundary Commission as long as IRA attacks on the north continued. Finally, there was a growing awareness on most sides that mutual consent rather than legal force was needed to solve the remaining issues of the Irish question. Added to this was a fear of reopening a Pandora's box and trying to enforce recommendations that could lead to further bloodshed. Political instability in Britain with three general elections and four governments between 1922 and 1924 also contributed to the delay.

It was not until June 1923, just after the end of the Irish Civil War and the defeat of the anti-Treaty IRA, that W. T. Cosgrave, executive president of the Irish Free State, informed Prime Minister Stanley Baldwin that a formal request was about to be made for Article 12 of the Treaty to be invoked and a Boundary Commission set up. From now on, Irish Free State policy on Northern Ireland was to be conducted by entirely peaceful means. The Free State government had already established its North-Eastern Boundary Bureau in October 1922 with Kevin O'Shiel, an Omagh solicitor, as assistant legal advisor. He advised the Free State government in 1923 that it was unrealistic to expect that, in the middle of a civil war, the Dublin government was strong enough to force the British Conservative government to accede to Irish demands. O'Shiel's Boundary Bureau was established to promote the Free State case, and so in July 1923 the south appointed Eoin MacNeill – a Gaelic scholar, former leader of the Irish Volunteers and current minister of education in the Free State government – as its boundary commissioner. Surprisingly, nobody in the Free State enquired how a full-time politician with a department to run could also have the time to take on the onerous work of a boundary commissioner involving, as it did, extended tours of the border towns of the north. By now the south had begun to realise that the Boundary Commission offered the best (and last) opportunity to at least amend, if not end, the border. While this possibility remained and many northern nationalists retained at least some hope of coming under Dublin rule, there was no incentive for the Free State to recognise Northern Ireland. Consequently, this hostile attitude from the Free State only intensified the traditional fears of the Ulster unionists and, in turn, made Northern Ireland even less likely to participate in the Boundary Commission. The Free State was in a very difficult position. It was coming under sustained criticism from northern nationalists questioning whether it was determined to push for the Boundary Commission to be set up, while at the same time it could not be seen as having closed the door on alternative strategies including, possibly, some suggested by Northern Ireland.

In early 1924, once the Free State had secured its territory after the end of the civil war and once it became likely that there would be a new government in Britain, Cosgrave came under increased pressure in the Dáil regarding the boundary issue. A possible tactic to force the issue was Ireland's admission to the League of Nations in September 1923; it was reasonable to expect that if nothing was done to overcome the deadlock created by the refusal of Northern Ireland to participate, then the Free State would appeal to the League. This was a situation British governments, both Conservative and Labour, wished to avoid.

The first Labour government in 1924 was therefore immediately confronted with the outstanding and still controversial issue of the Boundary Commission. Labour was reluctant to constitute the Commission and only did so after repeated attempts to bring about a compromise between north and south had failed. In particular, the government wished to avoid the inevitable controversy it believed the Boundary Commission would cause, irrespective of its eventual recommendations. During its ten months in power, the Labour government attempted three times to persuade both Irish states to reach an agreed solution without the necessity of establishing a Commission at all. Labour invited both Craig and Cosgrave to a conference on the issue in early February. There now commenced a theatrical three-way process which was to dominate the first British Labour administration. The government was determined to prove that it was as responsible as its predecessors in delivering the terms of the Anglo-Irish Treaty, even though it would have preferred an informal solution over employing the whole panoply of convening the Boundary Commission as required by the Treaty. The new Free State government, now in control of all of its territory, was anxious to see the Boundary Commission implemented in order to deflect political criticism from anti-Treaty republicans that it was less than robust in defending Irish nationalist interests. The northern government remained characteristically stubborn, obstructive and obdurate until the end. The British government considered bypassing the Boundary Commission and, instead, utilising Article 14 of the Treaty – which allowed an all-Ireland council to be set up that could deal with the thorny issue – but Northern Ireland rejected this proposal unambiguously as, subsequently, did the Free State. The British government was acutely aware that, in effect, it could not refuse what previous British governments had agreed to.

The conference was adjourned on 2 February to meet again within twenty-eight days, whereupon Craig fell ill, but the Northern Ireland government had already indicated that it would refuse to appoint a commissioner if and when the Boundary Commission was constituted. It also argued that it would refuse to accept the decisions of the Boundary Commission unless all decisions of the Commission were unanimous, whereas the Free State would only proceed if majority verdicts were accepted. Finally, the British government sought legal advice as to whether two commissioners could constitute the Boundary Commission if Britain and the Free State appointed commissioners and Northern Ireland did not. The only step Britain was able to take was the appointment of Sir Richard Feetham, a South African High Court judge, as chairman of the Boundary Commission. It was obvious that the Unionists were using delaying tactics, hoping for a Conservative government in the near future. Subsequent meetings of the conference failed to take place, as it was apparent that there was little chance of agreement being reached on settling the boundary without recourse to the official establishment of the Boundary Commission. As a result, the Free State promptly demanded official confirmation of the Commission. Meanwhile, the British government had been informed that the Commission would not be legal if Northern Ireland refused to appoint a commissioner, and so amending legislation would have to be introduced to ensure that the Commission was legally constituted. At the same time, the Judicial Committee of the Privy Council was asked if the Commission was valid without a Northern Ireland commissioner and whether the British government could make an appointment on behalf of Northern Ireland. Meanwhile, the chairman of the putative Boundary Commission, Chief Justice Feetham, also asked the Privy Council to rule whether decisions could be made unanimously or by a majority vote as well as whether the chairman would have a casting vote.

At the end of July the Privy Council ruled that without a representative from Northern Ireland the Boundary Commission would be invalid, but, if all three appointments were made, a majority would rule. It became apparent that the introduction of a one-clause bill as an amendment to the Treaty would have to be introduced to enable the Boundary Commission to function, and that this needed to be ratified by both Dublin and London. This would involve London nominating a representative for Northern Ireland with all subsequent decisions being based on a majority rather than a unanimous vote.

The Labour government was acutely aware that if it could be seen to be amending the 1921 Treaty, the Irish Free State could do so too. There was a danger of provoking renewed violence on either side of the border, which could even result in the overthrow of the Free State government. On the other hand, the British government was also aware that even the threat of constitutional upheaval in Ireland was outweighed by the constitutional consequences of what might happen in Britain, including the defeat of the government and its replacement by a new government unsympathetic to the Free State. The British concern was that any attempt to push through the amending legislation quickly (which is what Cosgrave and the Free State government were arguing for) could alienate a House of Lords that retained substantial residual support for the Ulster unionists.

In the event, the Irish Free State (Confirmation of Agreement) Bill was introduced into the House of Commons on 6 August 1924. Dáil Éireann considered similar legislation shortly afterwards, where it was pointed out that if one aspect of the Treaty could be amended the Dáil was now free to amend other parts of the Treaty and, in effect, totally rewrite the constitution of the Irish Free State. That the whole Treaty could unravel was one of the great fears, not only of the Labour government but of the entire British political class. At the end of September the Irish Free State (Confirmation of Agreement) Bill received its second reading at Westminster. The Conservative opposition stopped short of opposing the Bill outright, as it did not want to precipitate a general election on the issue of the Boundary Commission. The Tories' major fear was that the Lords would reject the Bill and thus cause an election on Ireland, which Baldwin feared his party might lose. Indeed, it was Baldwin who persuaded Craig to moderate opposition to the Bill and to accept the British nomination for the Northern Ireland commissioner.

The Irish Free State (Confirmation of Agreement) Act therefore received royal assent on 9 October 1924, by which time the government had appointed a Northern Ireland representative to the Commission. J. R. Fisher was a barrister and former editor of the *Northern Whig** and, as such, was

---

* A daily liberal unionist paper based in Belfast.

sympathetic to northern unionist political sensibilities. Once the British parliament had confirmed the amending legislation, the Free State reciprocated in mid-October by passing the Treaty (Confirmation of Supplemental Agreement) Bill. But by the end of the month, Labour's first experiment in government had ended with general election defeat, and a Conservative government with its largest majority since 1832 took power under Stanley Baldwin. So, although all the preparation involved in establishing the Boundary Commission had taken place during Labour's short tenure in power, the Commission was only fully constituted on 29 October – the day of the general election when Labour lost office.

The controversy over the Boundary Commission had come at exactly the same time as one of the most politically turbulent periods in British political history. Once the Tories returned to power in 1922 after the overthrow of Lloyd George and the coalition government, Conservative criticism of the Treaty provisions as they affected Ulster extended to those Conservative ministers in the former government, such as Austen Chamberlain and Lord Birkenhead. This criticism came most vituperatively from the die-hard traditionalists who, although not as influential as they had once been, regarded the Treaty clauses on finance and the boundary as an unacceptable betrayal of Ulster. This element of the Conservative Party saw the Treaty as an outrageous placation of the enemies of the British Empire, and this undoubtedly resulted in renewed impetus to the right wing, which led not only to the rejection of Lloyd George but also their own leaders in the coalition. The effects of all this were felt beyond Bonar Law's brief tenure as prime minister and were still potent when his replacement, Stanley Baldwin, was attempting to reunite his party after the traumas of the coalition experience. For a time, therefore, it seemed that the Tories would split on the one remaining issue of the Irish question: the future of the Irish border.

The political demise of Lloyd George in 1922, when the Conservatives abandoned the coalition, meant that the author of both the Government of Ireland Act and the Anglo-Irish Treaty was no longer at the centre of political power in Britain. Ironically, given the subsequent criticism of both pieces of legislation, these measures were intended ultimately to bring about a united Ireland and the abolition of the border, although many Irish nationalists failed to interpret the situation this way at the time. Lloyd George's successors – Bonar Law, Stanley Baldwin and Labour's Ramsay MacDonald – did not share his ultimate ambition of Irish reunification. They regarded the removal of all traces of the Irish problem from the centre of British political life as being the prime essential requirement. Between 1922 and 1925 all three British prime ministers, suspicious of the continued propensity of Ireland to create havoc in British politics, embarked upon a policy of delay and obfuscation, particularly on the constitution of the Boundary Commission, as they were all aware of the combustible sensitivity of this issue in particular. The net effect was to undermine those aspects of the Treaty that were meant to facilitate eventual Irish reunification. These delaying tactics were likewise exacerbated by the Northern Ireland government's outright refusal, in defiance of the terms of the Treaty, to nominate its boundary commissioner. What's more, the Irish Civil War prevented the Irish Free State from demanding the implementation of the Boundary Commission; the continued political violence south of the border was hardly a recommendation for the suitability of a state that could not control all of its territory taking over that of its neighbour as well.

Baldwin's inertia was thus facilitated by the disarray within Irish nationalism. The civil war in the south not only split former republican comrades but also divided northern nationalists to perhaps an even greater – albeit not so murderous – extent. In addition to the division between the pro- and anti-Treaty elements of nationalism, there was a split between the old Irish Nationalist Party, which was still electorally strong in the north, and Sinn Féin. Finally, there was a difference in outlook between border nationalists – optimistic about transfer to the Free State under the Boundary Commission recommendations – and urban nationalists in Belfast, who realised that no matter what recommendations the Boundary Commission might make, they would be remaining in Northern Ireland.

In summary, in 1924 the Irish Free State, once more in control of its territory after defeating the anti-Treaty republicans in the civil war, demanded that Britain's new Labour government finally constitute the Boundary Commission. However, Sir James Craig's refusal once more to appoint a northern commissioner caused anxiety in Westminster at the prospect of Ireland returning to the centre of British political life. Labour's subsequent decision to amend the original Irish Free State (Agreement) Act ran the risk of reopening the whole debate on Ireland at Westminster, particularly in the Conservative-dominated House of Lords with its residual sympathy for Ulster unionism – and Baldwin, as leader of the opposition, feared that any Labour attempt to bypass Northern Ireland would be likely to be thrown out by the Tory Lords. In the event, Baldwin managed to prevail upon sufficient Conservative members of the Lords not to vote down MacDonald's amending legislation, the approval of which enabled the Boundary Commission to be established and finally carry out its work in 1925.

6

The Recommendations of the
Irish Boundary Commission

The work of the Irish Boundary Commission in 1924 and 1925 occupies a paradoxical position in Anglo-Irish history in the twentieth century. It was the only example of the post-war reordering of international boundaries, so in vogue after the Treaty of Versailles, to take place in the United Kingdom; it also marked the beginning of a partition process similarly implemented by the British in further flung parts of the Empire, such as Palestine and India. And yet its recommendations were summarily buried by all three governments in London, Belfast and Dublin. This burial should not detract from the fact that these governments' reactions to the Boundary Commission proposals mark the end of Britain's direct involvement in Irish politics 125 years after the Act of Union. The irony is that for an exercise whose work and recommendations were swiftly obliterated – thus forcing the three governments involved to pragmatically readopt the county boundaries of the Government of Ireland Act as the border – it had so much impact on the course of Irish history for the next century. Article 12 of the Anglo-Irish Treaty, which established a provision for the Boundary Commission, may have been either deliberately ambiguous or simply casually drafted, but the stifled recommendations of the Commission in 1925 certainly more effectively, in most cases at least, reflected the wishes of local inhabitants than the belatedly reconfirmed six-county border. It is a sobering thought that it could be argued that more than two hundred lives might have been saved between 1969 and the mid-1990s if the Boundary Commission's recommendation that South Armagh be transferred to the Free State had been enacted.

From that perspective, the Irish Boundary Commission is of major significance. It has generally been regarded as a failure because its proposals were ignored by the governments concerned and, as a result of this neglect, has been overshadowed in the history of Anglo-Irish relations. But the meticulous nature of the research alone makes it a document of historical importance, irrespective of the response to its recommendations, and the fact that its findings were kept secret for over forty years is further testament to its historical and political import.

The proposal for a Boundary Commission, as laid out in Article 12 of the Anglo-Irish Treaty of 1921, was not part of a planned British policy to partition Ireland. If anything, that had already been achieved by the Government of Ireland Act of the previous year, which had established two Home Rule parliaments in Ireland. Instead, Lloyd George during the Treaty negotiations found himself in a difficult position. Even though the Treaty proposals aspired to the ultimate unity of Ireland (and, as a result, included Northern Ireland inside the Irish Free State unless it decided to opt out) Lloyd George was sensitive to his Tory colleagues' insistence that on no account should Northern Ireland be coerced into a united Ireland. The proposal for a Boundary Commission was a device to recognise Northern Ireland's right to secede from the Irish Free State while at the same time reassuring the Sinn Féin delegates of the essential integrity of Ireland. Article 12 was thus, in essence, a device to get over the very real possibility of the Treaty negotiations collapsing. The article was very vaguely worded – perhaps deliberately so. It made no reference to the time period by which the Commission had to meet and report (in the event, the Commission met more than three years after the Treaty proposed it). It made no reference as to how it should be comprised and how its research should be carried out. In addition, the term 'Northern Ireland' was determined to be the six territorial counties defined by the Government of Ireland Act, which means that even to this day there are no defined political borders in either Lough Foyle or Carlingford Lough. The fact that its terms of reference were so vague enabled Lloyd George to at least give the impression to Irish nationalists that it could potentially recommend sufficient changes to make Northern Ireland constitutionally unviable while at the same time suggesting to unionists that only minor rectification of the border would take place. In the event, given its lack of focus, it gave great responsibility and power to the chairman to decide these specific terms of reference. The appointed chairman, Sir Richard Feetham, decided that his responsibility was to make recommendations in accordance with the situation in which the Boundary Commission found itself in 1924–5, given that Northern Ireland had been in existence for over four years by that time and had been increasingly stable over that period.

He also argued that after any new boundary was established Northern Ireland must still be recognisable as the 'same provincial entity'* as before and that under no circumstances would he countenance the transfer of any substantial town, irrespective of the wishes of its population. Feetham was facilitated in his decision-making by the fact that there had recently been so many short-lived British governments, each with widely differing views on their preferred outcome of the Commission, and by the fact that this was the first time any British government had considered any concept so European as the implementation of partition. In that context, Northern Ireland is one of the few states still surviving from the post-1918 redrawing of European boundaries. The Irish Boundary Commission allowed all the competing parties involved to abdicate their own responsibilities on partition, thus allowing someone else (Feetham) to make the inevitable compromise. Furthermore, the partition of Ireland was not like other partitions in Europe where whole populations were forced to leave as a result of where the boundary was placed. In Ireland the proposal was the opposite: to shift the boundary to accommodate the desires of the majority of the population with no expectation that anyone would have to move. In addition, in his desire to determine the boundary based on the market areas of each small town, Feetham failed to recognise that constant improvements in communications, transport and urbanisation would, over time, inevitably change the nature of market areas of between five and ten miles around towns. In effect, Feetham was proposing boundary changes that would

---

*As noted in the Boundary Commission report.

be fossilised in the mid-1920s with no contingency for future amendment if needed. Any political change in the border area would inevitably result in at least some population movement – and, indeed, this is what happened, as many Protestants along the border moved east after partition. But Feetham's recommendations, based on the wishes of local inhabitants, were determined solely on a census already nearly fifteen years old by 1925, with no awareness that the implementation of such recommendations would itself have consequences. As a further example, within a few years the railway system on which so much of this was based began to be rationalised so that, in effect, the Boundary Commission's recommendations designed a border for an Ireland that within fifty years would have changed beyond all recognition.

The Boundary Commission was the final postscript before Ireland and the Irish border were finally removed from British – or, more specifically, Westminster – politics. Although all the preparation involved in establishing the Boundary Commission had taken place during Labour's short period in office as a minority government, which ended in November 1924, the Commission met for the first time in London later that month, shortly after Stanley Baldwin's Conservative administration had replaced Labour. It had a preliminary tour of the border area in December 1924, sampling opinion and gathering initial evidence. It first met in Northern Ireland at Armagh on 9 December 1924 where it spent its first three nights. It then spent another three nights each at Enniskillen, Newtownstewart and Derry. Already it was becoming apparent that these were border areas, and nationalists from further afield – from eastern Tyrone, for instance – were commenting on this, stating that it was obvious that only those districts adjacent to the border were going to be considered. The Commission met with members from county councils in Armagh, Monaghan, Fermanagh, Tyrone and Londonderry and with town councillors from Armagh, Monaghan, Newry, Enniskillen, Omagh, Strabane and Derry. It also met His Majesty's Lieutenants in each county, MPs, ecclesiastical dignitaries and senior police officers in Armagh, Down, Monaghan, Fermanagh, Tyrone, Derry and Donegal as well as representatives from local political organisations. It spent a substantial part of the following year travelling around Northern Ireland receiving submissions. The Commission was nothing if not thorough: between March 1925 and the following July it heard 575 witnesses representing fifty-eight groups and public bodies and ten individuals. It resumed sittings for hearing evidence at Armagh between 3 and 7 March and again on 19 March, at the Great Northern Hotel at Rostrevor on 9 March and then a suspension for the Northern Ireland parliamentary elections on 3 April. Between 22 April and 6 May it met at Killyhevlin near Enniskillen, and from 14 May to 5 June at its offices at 1 St Columb's Court, Derry, and then at Knocknamoe, Omagh, from 6 June to 2 July. The Commission received evidence from customs both in Northern Ireland and in the Irish Free State as well as the portal inspector of the Port of Londonderry, the local manager of Cross-Channel Steamship Services in Derry and the chairman of the Lough Erne Drainage Board. The British and Northern Ireland governments declined to make representations to the committee, but the Irish Free State government empowered legal counsel to meet the Commission on 4 and 5 December 1924 in order to outline the Free State interpretation of the powers of the Boundary Commission. The Commission also received witnesses from the Free State on statistics and other matters on 25 August 1925.

As early as 1924, it was clear even to elements inside the Free State government that, given its remit and composition, the Commission's final report would hardly contain recommendations that would undermine the viability of the northern state. It became obvious that, when the previous Labour government had appointed Feetham as chairman of the Boundary Commission and J. R. Fisher as the Northern Ireland commissioner, this was reassuring from the north's perspective and ominous for the Free State. Furthermore, the southern reaction to the appointment of the three boundary commissioners was extremely lax and passive. Although all commissioners agreed a policy of secrecy in which they would not speak to outsiders regarding the work of the Commission, it became apparent through the course of its investigations that Fisher was providing regular reports to Craig, while the Free State commissioner, MacNeill, refused to keep his colleagues in the south similarly informed of developments. Neither the Free State nor indeed the other boundary commissioners questioned Fisher about his obvious abuse of trust, nor did Dublin seek to elicit information on progress from their representative, who appeared to believe that he was on a legal rather than a political mission. It is also at least arguable that MacDonald had appointed Feetham in order to avoid criticism from the right, as he knew that Feetham was an imperialist who had close contacts with prominent Conservatives, particularly on the future role of the Empire. MacDonald also understood that Fisher's previous career as editor of the unionist-supporting *Northern Whig* would at least assuage unionist suspicions. When Feetham stated categorically at the beginning of his work that the wishes of the inhabitants would be overruled by economic and geographic conditions, it became clearly apparent to all, except those in the Free State who myopically refused to believe it, that the Boundary Commission was not going to be both the author of the extinction of Northern Ireland and the midwife of Irish unity. Feetham's reference to a redetermined boundary with Northern Ireland also implied that there would still be a Northern Ireland with which to have a boundary. As soon as the Commission was formally constituted, Feetham suggested that Craig and Cosgrave meet once more to try to resolve the issue without the extensive panoply of the Commission being invoked. However, as Cosgrave was now under intense pressure in the Free State for the Boundary Commission to progress, it was obvious that the time for informal meetings of this kind had passed. Apart from a Free State proposal for a plebiscite in all the Poor Law Unions* in the north that had shown a Catholic majority in the previous census in 1911 and which was ignored by Feetham, the entire Boundary Commission machinery was then mobilised.

The Free State's publicity unit – the North-Eastern Boundary Bureau – submitted maximum and minimum claims to the Boundary Commission. The maximum claim would still have left a viable northern state around its Greater Belfast heartland, although the whole issue of geographical viability

---

* Poor Law Unions were areas established under the Poor Relief (Ireland) Act in 1838 and were responsible for the administration of poor relief.

was academic, as the north's economic viability depended upon its status as part of the United Kingdom and that country's willingness to finance its continued existence. The Free State's position was further undermined by a lack of consensus amongst northern Catholics themselves. Those living in the Greater Belfast area preferred to see as many of their co-religionists as possible remaining inside a truncated Northern Ireland; furthermore, nationalists' proposals that their particular townland on the border should be transferred to the Free State, thus moving the border further east and north, were not embraced with much enthusiasm as a coherent nationalist approach. The Free State's maximum claim would have put over a quarter of a million Protestants inside the Free State against their will, and even the minimum claim envisaged 179,000 northern Protestants transferred and still left 266,000 Catholics marooned on the wrong side of the border. However, all of this was theoretical as long as Article 12 stated that the course of the boundary was to be qualified according to economic and geographic interests. The financial arguments used by the Ulster unionists struck a real chord with Feetham. In effect, the chairman of the Boundary Commission had made it clear that, in his view, the main elements of the Free State's case – that the Commission was empowered to make sweeping territorial changes based on conditions as they were in 1921, that a plebiscite should be held in the border region and that it had no mandate to transfer territory from the south to the north – were incorrect. Furthermore, in April 1923, when the boundary was still being entrenched but its final position had yet to be determined, the Free State added status to the new boundary through defining its functional dimension by imposing a customs barrier. Quite remarkably, this Act preceded the final demarcation of the border and was enacted by a political entity totally opposed to having a border at all. It is a classic example of boundary administration actually pre-dating the final boundary delimitation. Clearly the south felt, erroneously as it turned out, that having a customs boundary in place would create sufficient economic hardship to persuade the north to be more malleable during the boundary discussions. By failing to reach agreement on the terms and conditions of Article 12 prior to the Boundary Commission being established, the Free State had effectively handed that responsibility to Richard Feetham, the British-appointed chairman.

The fact that scrutiny of what Article 12 of the Treaty actually meant took place at the end of the process rather than before was typical of the vagueness surrounding the whole proposal ever since it first appeared in the Anglo-Irish Treaty in 1921. Its terms of reference were determined by the Commission itself or, more specifically, by Feetham as its chair. It was Feetham who took the lead on questioning witnesses and challenging evidence, and the other two commissioners were quite prepared to allow this to become the pattern for the conduct of proceedings. It was Feetham who, in effect, stated in the Boundary Commission report that as Northern Ireland must at the end of the process remain 'the same provincial entity', the principle of maintaining territorial integrity should be considered superior to that of discharging the principle of self-determination of peoples. In essence, Feetham overturned the principle of deciding the future of the boundary based on the wishes of the people who lived there – a principle that had already, in the context of the Irish border, been undermined by the insistence in the Treaty of the significance of the consideration of economic and geographic issues.

Feetham interpreted, in direct contrast to the Free State government, Article 12 as facilitating a two-way transfer of territory. He also quite peremptorily dismissed the whole concept of plebiscites, simply because there was no mention of such in the Treaty. In this he was in tune with successive British governments, which distrusted the prospect of using plebiscites in Ireland because of the likelihood of inflaming tensions, irreparably dividing Irish opinion and negating whatever chances there were of eventual Irish unity. He also qualified Article 12's commitment to the significance of the wishes of the people in determining the course of the boundary by stating that simple majorities would not suffice. He accepted the 1911 census as the key source of the wishes of the people, even though considerable change had taken place between 1911 and 1925, and made the automatic assumption that all Protestants would like to live in Northern Ireland and all Catholics would prefer to live in the Irish Free State. Finally, the importance he attached to – particularly in the case of Newry and the surrounding areas – unionist representations on the significance of economic conditions meant that these representations made through witnesses at the Commission in 1925 were far more up to date than the wishes of the inhabitants as exemplified by census figures a decade and a half out of date. He attached a great deal of weight to the smallest of demographic units such as district electoral divisions, which were not historical or geographical divisions, and even went as far as splitting townlands (the smallest form of administrative unit) for inclusion in separate jurisdictions rather than recognising the significance of county boundaries; although, conversely, he understood that Northern Ireland should be recognised as a unit with its own parliament and government. He demanded substantial majorities for change and, even then, these were subject to the qualifications of economic and geographic conditions. The wonder is that Free State commissioner Eoin MacNeill acquiesced in all of this.

Feetham and the Boundary Commission concentrated on four specific geographic areas: Co. Tyrone; Co. Fermanagh and portions of southern Tirconnail (Donegal) and south-west Monaghan; Londonderry and north-east Donegal; and Co. Armagh, eastern Monaghan and Co. Down. In all of these certain factors were taken as given: Protestants were regarded as the chief contributors to the rates with Roman Catholics often described as 'labourers and farm servants' contributing little or nothing to the same. Protestant submissions often complained that they were permanently based men of property, whereas many Catholics were temporary labourers working seasonally. In an age when all men had just been enfranchised, the rights of property were still regarded as almost as important as the rights of man. As such, it followed that consideration of economic and geographic conditions were at least more likely to be, on balance, more sensitive to the concerns of the local Protestant population given that the Commission regarded that community as having more of a financial stake in the local economy than their Catholic neighbours. The investigations into the more rural case studies were certainly less problematic than the controversies surrounding the Derry and Newry areas, with the emphasis there on the deciding significance of economic and geographic factors. Once the Commission indicated that it did not regard county boundaries as sacrosanct when it came to redrawing the border, it was obvious that there was an undeniable logic both on demographic, economic and geographic grounds for the transfer of the vast expanse of moorland west of Killeter in Co. Tyrone and the mountainous country of South Armagh to the Free State. The other smaller border readjustments (with the notable anomaly of east Donegal) were simply reduced versions of the above. Although the Commission did not expressly state that it regarded proposed areas for transfer to be contiguous to the existing border, it refused to consider for transfer Protestant areas in Monaghan and, to a lesser extent, Cavan, as these scattered Protestant communities were separated from their brethren in Northern Ireland by a substantial ring of Catholic territory. There was little chance then of nationalist Magherafelt in east Derry or Downpatrick in east Down (the furthest areas from the Free State asking to be considered for transfer) of having their representations seriously considered. By steering the work of the Commission to existing border areas only, the commissioners skilfully avoided having to confront the reality that one-third of the population of Northern Ireland was nationalist – as was half of its territory.

Derry and Newry were fully expected to be transferred to the Free State. With Catholic populations of 56 per cent in Derry and 75 per cent in Newry, according to the 1911 census, nationalists expected and unionists feared that both would be recommended for transfer. Both sides knew that the Catholic population of Derry had increased substantially since 1911 as a result of Catholic immigration from Donegal to work in the city's factories during the economically prosperous period of the First World War. In addition, Derry was the principal port for the entire north-west of Ireland. Newry, on the other side of Northern Ireland, was in a broadly similar position, but, it was argued, whereas Derry was economically significant for the entire north-west of the island of Ireland, Newry was one of only four small ports (the others being Warrenpoint, Greenore and Dundalk) serving a smaller area than Derry. Furthermore, Newry's economy was geared geographically through river valleys to the north and east to Portadown and Belfast rather than through the mountainous barrier to Dundalk in the south.

Derry was, however, in one unique respect distinct from all other areas along the border: symbolically and politically, it was the foundation of Protestant resistance in Ireland to the forces of Irish Catholicism. The significance of the Siege of Derry in 1689 had persuaded the new Unionist rulers of Northern Ireland to determine that they would never allow the city to be transferred out of their jurisdiction.

The Commission received the following representations in Derry:

- A committee of nationalist inhabitants of the City of Londonderry stressing economic connections with Donegal and requesting the transfer of the whole city to the Free State (or else adopting the River Foyle as the new border).
- A committee of nationalist inhabitants of the Londonderry Poor Law Union asking for the transfer of the city

and the surrounding Londonderry No. 1 Rural District Council to the Free State.

- The City Corporation of Londonderry, which stressed the trade links to the rest of Northern Ireland and the Protestant population of east Ulster; that the Government of Ireland Act stated that Derry was part of Northern Ireland and that no part of the city touches the border; and that transfer would damage industry. It also called for a readjustment of the Donegal border in favour of Northern Ireland.
- The Honourable the Irish Society, which argued that Lough Foyle was entirely in Northern Ireland.
- Londonderry Port and Harbour commissioners, who were prepared to accept small readjustments of the border.
- Londonderry members of the Shirt and Collar Manufacturers Federation stressing that both imports of raw materials and exports were mainly from and to Britain.
- The Co. Donegal Protestant Registration Association wanting unionist districts in Donegal (Londonderry No. 2 Rural District Council and Strabane No. 2 Rural District Council) to be transferred to Northern Ireland.
- A group of Co. Donegal businessmen who wanted either all of Derry or the west bank transferred to the Free State and were opposed to parts of Donegal being transferred to Northern Ireland.

Out of sixty-one witnesses from east Donegal, fifty-four complained about the customs barrier between themselves and Derry; forty-six of these said that they wished to be on the same side of the border as Derry, and the remaining eight said the same about Strabane. In this case, at least, it appeared that economic and geographic considerations and the wishes of the inhabitants were the same.

The Boundary Commission rejected the transfer of the city and the liberties (the area between the city and the border) to the Irish Free State on the basis that this would have to include the Protestant east bank of the Foyle as well. Clearly, the wishes of the inhabitants in this respect were not taken into account and nor were economic and geographic factors, given that it was estimated that 75 per cent of Derry's trade was with the Irish Free State. The clue to recognising the reasons behind the decision lies in Feetham's original resolution not to consider entire counties as candidates for transfer. If the Boundary Commission had recommended the transfer of both Tyrone and Fermanagh to the Free State, the case for Derry transferring also would have been easier. Feetham believed that, in the absence of Tyrone and Fermanagh transferring, the transfer of Derry would exacerbate a new series of economic misfortunes for the city, Tyrone and Fermanagh and also Co. Londonderry. Feetham's conclusion was that an attempt to remedy existing difficulties by transfer would make economic conditions worse rather than better, and it would damage the shirt industry on which 50 per cent of the city's population was dependent, as the industry relied upon an export trade to England and English factories. A political border along the Foyle was also rejected, as such economic and geographic division was unacceptable, even though it would have separated Catholic and Protestant parts of the city. The transfer of that part of east Donegal with Protestant majorities to Northern Ireland was approved as long as the railway line linking Inishowen to the rest of the Free State was maintained, as it was believed that removing boundary disruption for farmers in east Donegal would reduce inconvenience and expense. Even after the Boundary Commission's deliberations, there was continued debate (there still is) as to whether Lough Foyle was part of Co. Londonderry. The Commission's solution was to draw the boundary down the deep-water channel to the south of Moville and then after that to declare that the navigation channel serving Derry only should be considered part of Northern Ireland.

In Newry, the division was between the wishes of the vast majority of the Catholic population in contrast to the economic and geographic arguments put forward by the largely Protestant business community. The argument for inclusion in the Free State was supported by Newry Poor Law Union and Kilkeel Poor Law Union, which consisted of Newry No. 2 Rural District Council (including Crossmaglen), Newry Urban District Council (UDC), Newry No. 1 Rural District Council, Warrenpoint UDC and Kilkeel Union. This proposal was submitted by Newry UDC and a committee of nationalist inhabitants of the Poor Law Unions of Newry and Kilkeel. In addition, Warrenpoint UDC argued for inclusion in the Free State, but this was opposed by a group of property owners, traders and residents in the town. The proposal for inclusion in the Free State was opposed by Kilkeel Board of Guardians, Newry Chamber of Commerce, Bessbrook Spinning Company, Belfast City Water Works Board, Portadown and Banbridge Water Works Board and Camlough Water Works Trustees.

The pro-Free State argument was that Newry, Warrenpoint

and the Rural Districts of Newry No. 1, Newry No. 2 (including Crossmaglen) and Kilkeel all had Catholic majorities; they had also all had nationalist majorities in elections since local government reform in Ireland in 1898, until they were supressed by the new Northern Ireland government in 1922 for declaring their allegiance to the Free State. They also argued that the parliamentary constituencies of South Armagh and South Down had always returned nationalist MPs as had Newry Town constituency up until its abolition in 1918.

In contrast, Newry Chamber of Commerce said that all of these areas mentioned were economically 'irrevocably united'* to the northern government and any transfer to the Free State would cause loss of trade, increased taxation and unemployment. Kilkeel Rural District Council (now controlled by unionists given the nationalist boycott) argued that trade connections were overwhelmingly with Belfast and few with the Free State; that Carlingford Lough was a natural boundary; and that the local government area contained principal reservoirs for Belfast, Portadown, Banbridge and other towns. Bessbrook Spinning Mill submitted evidence that turned out to be very influential on the Boundary Commission, arguing that it was essentially a Northern Irish industry with little connection to the Irish Free State. Goods produced were sent to Belfast and other northern centres from which it received its raw materials and machinery. An intervening customs barrier would mean more delay, additional taxation and expense and would separate the industry from its natural base in Belfast.

---

*The Newry Chamber of Commerce's submission to the Irish Boundary Commission.

Three spinning or weaving mills in Newry employed seven hundred people, and three hundred Newry people worked at Bessbrook, three miles away. All trade was with Belfast, London and Scotland. A further 2,500 people worked at Bessbrook, so the total working in textiles in the Newry area was 3,200. The Commission accepted the argument that the industry was a Northern Irish one with very little contact with the Free State and also accepted that the introduction of a customs barrier would add difficulties including the possibility of different legislation, both financial and industrial, being introduced. Bessbrook Mills argued that it would prefer a customs barrier with Newry rather than with the rest of Northern Ireland.

The Port of Newry was controlled by Newry Port and Harbour Board, which argued that the port was irrevocably bound to Northern Ireland, particularly Armagh, Banbridge and Portadown. The coal trade, it argued, would be severely curtailed if Newry were to be transferred to the Free State, and there would be no alternative economic hinterland in the south to replace its existing one. Its trade in grain and food-stuffs was the port's only trade of importance with the Irish Free State, but the areas served could also be readily accessible from Dundalk. There was also debate on whether investment in port channels would be more likely from the north, which saw Newry as the main port for south-east Northern Ireland, or from the south, which may see it as a rival to Dundalk or Greenore.

In its conclusions, the Boundary Commission agreed that these economic factors precluded the transfer of Newry to the Irish Free State. There was also another factor, unique to

Newry's rural hinterland, and that was that the water supply to Belfast and other northern urban centres was sourced in the Mourne Mountains twenty miles from Newry, although it is highly significant that work only started here in 1923. The Belfast City and District Water commissioners had argued that the reservoirs were situated far from Newry in the middle of the Mourne Mountains and were separated from the town by a natural boundary, Carlingford Lough. There would be, they argued, an increased risk of attack on installations if the reservoirs were transferred south, and having Belfast's water located in the Free State would make its production more expensive. The Boundary Commission had severe concerns about these reservoirs being located in a foreign jurisdiction and the anxiety and insecurity this would cause in Belfast. In this it departed from the interpretation of the Irish Free State, which argued that economic and geographic concerns should only apply to the residents of any particular area rather than taking into account the inconvenience of city dwellers living over thirty miles away.

Newry was a significant market town and distributive hub as well as being an important industrial centre and port. Its population was three-quarters Catholic and its surrounding hinterland even more so. Arguably, on the basis of the wishes of the local population, Newry was a prime candidate for transfer to the Free State, but this was a classic example of the tension and potential incompatibility between demographic wishes as opposed to economic and geographic factors. The Boundary Commission believed that the economic interests of Newry were bound up with the industrial life of Northern Ireland and to sever this would lead to economic disaster.

Newry's links, it argued, were via river valleys to the north (as evidenced by the course of the Newry Canal to Portadown and Belfast) rather than through the mountains to the south. It accepted that a customs barrier between Newry and Belfast would wreck the Newry and Bessbrook textiles trades of flax-spinning and linen-weaving, damaging Newry as a centre for retail trade and as a market centre for agricultural produce from the surrounding areas.

This was the clearest example in the whole Boundary Commission report of the conflicts contained within Article 12 of the Anglo-Irish Treaty. The overwhelming wish of the local population that the area should be transferred to the Irish Free State was obviously incompatible with economic and geographic considerations, and, according to Article 12 as interpreted by the Boundary Commission, the latter must prevail.

On 7 November 1925 the conservative *Morning Post* newspaper published what it purported to be the final recommendation of the Irish Boundary Commission. If this report was correct, this truly amounted to an auspicious moment as, according to the terms of the Anglo-Irish Treaty, the official recommendations of the Boundary Commission would automatically become the new boundary between Northern Ireland and the Irish Free State without the need for enabling parliamentary legislation. The *Morning Post* article, while not totally correct in its predictions, did publish a map which for the first time indicated that the Free State was expected to surrender some territory, most notably in east Donegal. The Commission had openly and consistently argued that their boundary review was a two-way process involving transfers of land in either direction. The Free State, however, had chosen not to listen. The Commission believed their duty, according to their interpretation of Article 12 of the Treaty, was to determine the course of the border and not to decide whether or not there should be a border. Not only was there no suggestion that large areas of Northern Ireland should be transferred to the Free State – to the extent, according to wishful southern thinking, that the northern state would become unviable – but the recommendation was, in essence, that the border should remain a tidied-up version of what had originally been demarcated in the Government of Ireland Act five years earlier. This would involve a net gain of twenty-five thousand Catholics for the south and two thousand Protestants for the north. However, the real shock and embarrassment to the Free State was that it was expected to relinquish parts of prosperous and Protestant east Donegal for impoverished and Catholic South Armagh. From an ideological and political perspective, the new state could not countenance the return to imperial control of liberated territory whose freedom had been won so recently and at such a price. All Irish nationalists, whether pro- or anti-Treaty, had never considered the possibility that its territory would be handed to the north; the south had always regarded the Boundary Commission as a device for, if not the reunification of Ireland, at least bringing as many Catholics as possible inside the Free State's jurisdiction. This was also the great concern of Ulster unionists and their Conservative allies, as they clearly feared a transfer of northern territory to the south, which is why they had been so angry with Lloyd George and those coalition Tories who had signed a treaty that included a clause which, as they saw it, threatened to surrender unionists to the mercies of the Free State.

It was clear to both the British and the Irish Free State governments that, if the *Morning Post* report was proven to be correct, it would likely result in the collapse of the government in the south and its replacement with an anti-Treaty republican–Irish Labour Party coalition. The consequences of this were as apparent to Baldwin's Conservative government as they had been for its Labour predecessor. Both governments had been acutely conscious of the sensitivity of the Boundary Commission report. In anticipation of it recommending at least some repartition proposals, civil servants from both Dublin and London had been meeting regularly throughout 1925. Consequently, both Cosgrave and Craig were summoned to London where, on 3 December 1925, there was unanimous agreement that the Boundary Commission report would be shelved (and kept secret until 1969) with the existing boundary reconfirmed permanently. In return, the Free State was absolved of its responsibility under Article 5 of the Anglo-Irish Treaty to pay the British exchequer £10 million a year as its share of the British national debt. In addition, the proposed Council of Ireland, which had been designed with ingenuity by Lloyd George a mere four years previously to facilitate Irish reunification, was dissolved. The irony is that this was a significantly partitionist solution that exclusively benefited the citizens of the Free State rather than addressing any of the concerns of their separated northern nationalist brethren.

Up until 1922, partition was largely an administrative inconvenience that had little impact on the lives of people. Even if to the vast majority in Ireland, including one-third of the north's own citizens, Northern Ireland lacked legitimacy, Sinn Féin had at least formally accepted partition when it agreed the Anglo-Irish Treaty. However, Article 12 raised the hopes of nationalists, as they believed that much of the northern territory would transfer to the Free State, leaving the remainder as an unviable rump. Although the Treaty included measures to ultimately normalise relationships between the two parts of Ireland in the short term, it achieved exactly the opposite. The uncertainty of the likely outcome of the Boundary Commission encouraged many nationalists in the north to continue to boycott the northern state and, of course, this response and the Boundary Commission itself just contributed to the growing paranoia of northern Protestants.

The publication of the *Morning Post* article led directly to the final Irish political crisis affecting London, Dublin and Belfast. The Irish Free State commissioner Eoin MacNeill resigned from the Commission on 20 November and was also forced to give up his Cabinet seat in Dublin as well. MacNeill had been fully aware of what was likely to be the Boundary Commission recommendations but had failed to keep his Free State Cabinet colleagues informed. The Free State president, W. T. Cosgrave, demanded to meet British ministers to point out forcibly that his government was likely to collapse if the Commission's award were implemented. Initially, Cosgrave and his deputy Kevin O'Higgins hoped for ameliorating measures that would benefit the northern minority. In return, the Free State would accept the existing boundary. O'Higgins was looking for concessions to 'deaden in the twenty-six counties the echo of the outcry of the Catholics of North-East Ulster'.* It was only when it

---

* Conference at the Treasury, Whitehall, 1 December 1925.

became apparent that Craig would release only thirty prisoners and was determined not to give ground on the future of the Special Constabulary, the restoration of proportional representation or the end to alleged gerrymandering of electoral districts, that attention turned to Article 5 of the Anglo-Irish Treaty. This was the clause that, by independent arbitration, was to determine the Free State's share of Britain's public debt, and originally it was determined by both sides to delay this until after the boundary issue was resolved. Now, in early December 1925, as a means of navigating through the Boundary Commission crisis, Cosgrave, Baldwin and Craig negotiated an agreement whereby the Free State agreed to pay compensation for property damage in both the War of Independence and the Civil War in return for Article 5 of the Treaty being dropped, thus saving the Free State from having to pay its share of the British national debt. Once negotiations began to concentrate on these financial questions, attention shifted away from the boundary and from the plight of northern nationalists. In addition, Craig promised to accept the recommendations of British officials as regards republican prisoners in Northern Ireland; the Council of Ireland, designed by Lloyd George to facilitate Irish reunification, was abolished and its powers relating to Northern Ireland transferred to Belfast; and, most importantly, the Irish boundary was to remain unchanged.

Feetham was extremely disappointed about the fate that awaited his report, particularly given the assiduous work that had gone into producing it. Officially, he could have published the report, but he was prevailed upon by Baldwin, Craig and Cosgrave not to do so.

The outcome of this Tripartite Agreement between Baldwin, Craig and Cosgrave was the Irish Free State (Confirmation of Agreement) Bill, which was considered by the House of Commons on 8 December 1925, almost four years to the day after the signing of the Anglo-Irish Treaty. Baldwin remained acutely aware of the danger of the unresolved Irish issue returning to British politics. His overriding concern was that if the Tripartite Agreement to confirm the existing boundary were to be rejected and the Boundary Commission report published, Craig might appeal to Conservative back-benchers on any of the outstanding issues that still concerned unionists. The threat for Baldwin was that, even though the influence of the die-hards inside the Tory party was not as strong as it had once been, a substantial number of Tory MPs still felt they had a residual obligation to Ulster unionists, and this might trump their loyalty to their own party leader.

The danger was less, however, than it had been the previous year, when all three main political parties were balanced relatively evenly in the House of Commons. The divisions in the Conservative Party over the Treaty, and over the level of loyalty to be shown to Ulster unionism, could have split the party in 1922 or 1923 if the boundary crisis had taken place at that time. An unpredictable general election result in 1924 on the issue of Ireland might have cost Baldwin the leadership of his party as well as energising Lloyd George and reviving a reunited Liberal Party. By 1925, however, emotions had calmed, and Baldwin had a much larger majority, which he could use to face down any opposition on Ireland. The scale of Baldwin's election victory in 1924 meant that, in reality, he could determine the ultimate outcome of the Boundary

Commission, as he faced no meaningful opposition from Labour, certainly none from the Liberals and, in truth, even less now from his own party. In terms of pragmatic politics, it was now in all the parties' strategic interests for the status quo to be accepted. Even Craig realised that the outcome had provided the stability and permanence that he and his Ulster unionists had been pressing for over the preceding ten years. In the event, the legislation was passed.

On 8 December 1925, after forty years, Ireland ceased to be a dominating political concern in Britain. The Tripartite Agreement also marked the Irish Free State's final acceptance of the reality of partition. Northern nationalists were now acutely aware of the obvious impotence of the Free State in being able to come to their assistance. The transfer of responsibility for Irish affairs from London to Dublin and Belfast, with a 310-mile border dividing the two Irelands, meant that Ireland was now removed from its pivotal position in British politics for the first time since the Act of Union in 1800.

7

Aftermath

The British parliament's approval of the Tripartite Agreement in December 1925 buried the Boundary Commission's recommendations and confirmed the course of the Irish border as that outlined in the Government of Ireland Act of 1920. With that, the Irish border was finally determined on a permanent basis. The Boundary Commission itself had been established by the Anglo-Irish Treaty in 1921 and, during the debate on the Government of Ireland Bill the previous year in 1920, Craig himself had raised the possibility of a Boundary Commission to determine the acceptability of a six- or nine-county Ulster. This may have led to the British understanding, erroneous as it turned out, that Craig would be receptive to the proposal. Craig's anxiety about the continued viability of Northern Ireland had also increased following the outcome of the April 1925 Northern Ireland general election under proportional representation as it increased the number of Labour MPs in the northern parliament. Craig was concerned that, unless welfare levels in Northern Ireland were increased to the level of Great Britain, there could be an alliance between Labour and Joseph Devlin's nationalists demanding that the northern state be abolished and direct rule from London restored.

Even before the Boundary Commission had reported, and just after the 1925 Northern Ireland election, nationalist MPs Devlin and T. S. McAllister ended their abstention and took their seats in the northern parliament. In addition, during the negotiations on the Tripartite Agreement in December 1925, Kevin O'Higgins indicated that the Free State would urge other northern nationalist MPs to take their seats in the Belfast parliament. When the Tripartite Agreement was signed, the nationalists on the border, most of whom had supported the Treaty and the southern government in the hope of transfers of territory to the south, became disillusioned with the Free State after its inability to successfully represent their interests during the discussions that led to the Tripartite Agreement. In contrast, the nationalists of east Ulster, who had never stood much chance of being transferred, saw this as their opportunity to enter the northern parliament. The effects of the Boundary Commission on northern nationalists was baleful. On the one hand, the border nationalists had believed for four years that there was a real opportunity of joining with the south; on the other, those living in Belfast and the east of the province knew that, even if redrawing the border was the outcome of the Boundary Commission, its proposals would certainly not include them. As the nationalists on the border interpreted Article 12 of the Treaty as an opportunity for incorporation into the Free State, they were lukewarm about active participation in a united nationalist movement intent on defending Catholic interests across Northern Ireland. These divergent views resulted in the nationalist minority remaining bitterly divided during the formative years of Northern Ireland. Whether a united nationalist minority could have extracted concessions from the new Unionist government is debatable, given Craig's intransigence and his deferral to extreme unionism, but it could have influenced both Free State and Westminster attitudes, despite both wishing to divest themselves of any lingering responsibility for the north. By March 1926, five of the ten nationalist MPs had taken their seats in the northern parliament, and by November 1927 all nationalist MPs had abandoned abstentionism. In May 1928, a new nationalist party had been established to replace the old Home Rule party. However, after de Valera, with his irredentist policy on the north, came to power in 1932 and Irish unity again became a central issue, nationalist MPs withdrew once more and returned to the issue of partition. Devlin withdrew from the northern parliament in 1932 and died in 1934. His withdrawal from politics and subsequent death marked the end of northern nationalists' forlorn attempts to play a meaningful part in the northern state.

In the south, the Tripartite Agreement was greeted with profound disappointment. Cosgrave and the Free State government had very real concerns that their administration could collapse on this issue, which is why both he and his deputy Kevin O'Higgins were so desperate to secure a deal with Britain and Belfast. Their commitment to Irish territorial integrity and to their fellow nationalists in the north was never on a par with that of Griffith and Collins only four years earlier and, in truth, the new and inexperienced leaders in the Free State were negotiating with British politicians – many of whom had experience dealing with Ireland going back to 1912. The new Free State leaders prioritised survival of the government and the maintenance of stability in the south above all else. In order for the agreement to be ratified in the Dáil, Cosgrave needed to be aware of what de Valera and his abstentionist Sinn Féin TDs (members of Dáil Éireann) intended to do as regards entering the Dáil and voting against the agreement. Despite lambasting the government over the allegation that northern nationalists had been sold out for financial reasons, de Valera himself suggested that negotiations should have involved bartering over the oath and the Crown instead. Either way, northern nationalists would still have been abandoned. In the event, de Valera refused to abandon the republican principle of not recognising the Free State, and so a very real opportunity of destroying the state they refused to recognise went by the board. De Valera argued that there were not sufficient numbers of abstentionist Sinn Féin TDs to overthrow the Free State government on this issue. However, what ultimately motivated Dublin was the same weariness that so marked Westminster politics on this issue: that the politics of the Irish border had for far too long dominated parliamentary time, and this was now an opportunity to get rid of it once and for all. To many of the politicians now running the Free State, the Tripartite Agreement was the green light they needed to justify the construction of a religiously and culturally homogeneous state in which 93 per cent of the population was Roman Catholic. This was a more attractive and more achievable prospect than a united Ireland that would contain within its borders recalcitrant Ulstermen of whatever religious description. This emphasis on the Gaelic tradition and deference to the Roman Catholic Church on all social and educational issues only exacerbated the cultural and political chasm that had opened up between the two parts of Ireland. To an increasingly partitionist Free State, it was easier to develop a functioning nationalist society (which was difficult enough for an impoverished small state emerging from a vicious internecine civil war to achieve) than to put energies into attracting and accommodating people in Northern Ireland, a fractious but substantial minority, especially as there was every expectation that a successful outcome to this effort would be highly unlikely.

At Westminster the final word was left to Winston Churchill, the one British politician who had been centrally involved in all the twists and turns of Ireland's tortuous history since the heady days of 1912 and who was so influential in determining the politics of the new Ireland since the Treaty in 1921. He returned to his well-worn theme on the significance of the Irish conflict and its propensity for disrupting British political life when he concluded that:

The whole life of Ulster was overhung by the anxiety and menace of this boundary question. These parishes of Fermanagh and Tyrone have been the cause of every dispute which has prevented previous Irish settlements. They were the obstacles which broke up the Buckingham Palace Conference on the very eve of the War, and everyone knows that only a year ago this boundary question very nearly became a disastrous and dominating issue in our political life in this country.*

---

* House of Commons, Hansard, 8 December 1925, vol. 189, col. 360.

That same evening, the Irish Free State (Confirmation of Agreement) Act was passed, and Ireland was no longer a dominating influence in British politics. There could hardly have been one MP from any political party who did not breathe a sigh of relief in agreeing with Churchill's sentiments.

Meanwhile, in Northern Ireland, Sir James Craig was basking in the enormity of what had been achieved. For the first time in fifteen years the security of Ulster's Protestants had been realised, and the north's boundaries permanently agreed by all sides. However, the partition settlement finally agreed in 1925 failed to deal with the unresolved and unreconciled position of one-third of the population of Northern Ireland: the northern nationalists. The Catholic population was too large to be incorporated into Northern Ireland society, but its very size raises the question of why there was no concerted effort to integrate more fully a defeated population in the light of Craig's quite magnificent victory. Craig made little attempt to be conciliatory. During the uncertainty caused by the threat of the Boundary Commission redrawing the borders of Northern Ireland, the paranoia and siege mentality of Ulster's Protestants began to grow. The prime concern was to secure and strengthen the border, and all political decisions were based on this premise. In this they were left to organise themselves both politically and in security terms by successive British governments. There was a widespread tendency to view one-third of the population – Ulster Catholics – as undependable and potentially treasonous, a view exacerbated by the determined policy of non-recognition of the northern jurisdiction by the Free State. Many nationalist-controlled authorities in the north enthusiastically embarked upon this policy of non-recognition, which was countered by the northern authorities sending in commissioners to run nationalist councils, and by April 1922 twenty-one nationalist councils in the north had been suspended. While the prospect of the Boundary Commission either amending or removing the border remained, political uncertainty continued to be very potent. In 1925, with the demise of the Boundary Commission and the consequent confirmation of the original partition line, an exhausted peace fell upon Ireland. However, there was no subsequent rapprochement or reconciliation between the two jurisdictions or between the peoples who lived inside them.

The legitimacy of Northern Ireland in the eyes of its Catholic population remained a constant problem. Partition and the establishment of the northern state had been a victory for unionists and a continuing reminder of their defeat by nationalists. From the start, the majority of the nationalist Catholic population in the north had refused to recognise the new government. Even when, after the demise of the Boundary Commission, nationalist MPs started to enter the northern parliament in the mid-1920s, they did so reluctantly, preferring to leave the role of official opposition to Labour rather than assume it themselves. Craig, in particular, had the foresight and common sense to recognise that the future stability of the state depended upon Catholic acceptance of that state, and his failure to achieve this in its formative years led ultimately to the abolition of the Northern Ireland government in the 1970s. Yet any attempts at reconciliation were constantly undermined by the sectarian nature of the state as well as by the permanent irredentism of its southern neighbour. Any gesture or sign of rapprochement between unionists and nationalists was interpreted by many unionists as an unnecessary concession to a traitorous and devious minority. Consequently, Craig and his ministers were constantly in fear of accusations of political backsliding and weakness by their own voters. Conversely, any attempt to pander to unionist supporters lay the government open to accusations of gerrymandering and discrimination. Southern animosity also contributed to nationalist reluctance to accept the northern regime. After the demise of the Boundary Commission, northern nationalist representatives started to take their seats in the northern parliament. However, when de Valera came to power in 1932, the influence of southern irredentism persuaded northern Catholic MPs to withdraw once again and to restart their campaign against partition.

Craig's overwhelming ambition was to maintain Northern Ireland's position in the United Kingdom and to buttress partition. In this he was single-minded and steadfast. After 1925, with the dismissal of the Boundary Commission and the certainty of Northern Ireland's position inside its 1920 borders confirmed, a magnanimous and far-sighted policy would have been to reach out to his Catholic fellow northerners. However, this never happened. Craig contributed substantially towards building and maintaining Northern Ireland's stability in the years between 1922 and 1925, but by then he seemed to consider that his major ambition – to keep Northern Ireland as a bulwark against a united Ireland and inside the United Kingdom – had been achieved, although he remained prime minister of Northern Ireland until 1940. His statement about Northern Ireland being 'a Protestant Parliament and a

Protestant State'* in 1934 may have been a rhetorical response to events in the south, but instead of making a comprehensive attempt to win over the nationalist minority by addressing their fears and apprehension, Craig preferred to maximise his own party's support and thus sustain Unionist control over Northern Ireland. The criticism of Craig is that he saw himself first as leader of the Ulster Unionist party rather than as prime minister of Northern Ireland and never attempted to persuade northern nationalists to participate fully either in the state or in government. After the mobilisation of Protestant fears and prejudices in order to create the state, the new northern government was either unwilling or unable (or both) to offer the hand of conciliation to the resentful but substantial Catholic minority inside that state. Craig consistently used the power of the state to further the interests of Protestantism and Unionism, and his unimaginative leadership of a stable Northern Ireland stood in stark contrast to the leadership and determination he showed during the unstable early years of its existence.

The underlying fact that the partition of Ireland was also the partition of the United Kingdom did not seem to trouble successive British governments or, indeed, the British people. In losing one-fifth of its territory after the First World War, the victorious United Kingdom lost a larger proportion of its territory than the defeated Germany. However, there was no irredentist movement in Britain for the recovery of the south of Ireland. The Irish question had been answered, and so it faded out of the sphere of British domestic politics. The

---

*Parliament of Northern Ireland, 24 April 1934, vol. 16, col. 1095.

palpable relief at the time that Ireland was off the British agenda was matched only by an equal measure of perplexity when it reappeared half a century later at the beginning of the Northern Ireland conflict. All British political parties accepted the new dispensation. Ireland, north and south, was now out of sight and out of mind, and British politicians intended to keep it that way. Neither Baldwin, Lloyd George nor MacDonald ever again dealt with the boundary issue. The only further contact either MacDonald or Baldwin had with Ireland was when Éamon de Valera, the new Irish Free State leader and former republican ideologue, sought to overturn the Anglo-Irish Treaty in the 1930s. De Valera's decision to unpick the Treaty through changes in legislation from 1932 to 1936 – by abolishing the Irish Senate, the Oath of Allegiance and the position of Governor-General – was greeted with equanimity by Britain and was a very real indication that the symbols of British imperialism that were so important in the 1920s had declined in significance ten years later as Empire metamorphosed into Commonwealth. Whereas, in 1922, Winston Churchill was threatening to reinvade the Free State if the anti-Treaty IRA was not confronted by the Free State government, no such threats were made fifteen years later when de Valera in effect tore up many of the underlying principles of the Anglo-Irish Treaty.

Legally, it was no longer possible for Britain to intervene in Ireland once more, as according to the 1931 Statute of Westminster, Dominions of equal importance in the new Commonwealth could enact or change legislation without reference to the British parliament. De Valera's constitutional changes were accompanied by the Anglo-Irish Trade War.

Britain imposed a 20 per cent duty on Free State agricultural products in retaliation for de Valera refusing to pay land annuities from financial loans that had been granted to Irish tenant farmers by various land acts passed by British governments prior to independence. The eventual 1938 settlement, which involved a one-off payment by Ireland to the British of £10 million, also involved the transference back to Irish sovereignty of the Treaty Ports that had been retained by the British under the Anglo-Irish Treaty to protect the western sea approaches. Neither this dispute nor the IRA campaign in Britain in 1939–40 in any way prompted discussion or debate in Britain on the Irish border. Unionist concern over de Valera's new Irish constitution and its territorial claim to Northern Ireland, added to fears that the future of partition would feature in the 1938 Anglo-Irish talks, prompted Craig to call a general election in January 1938. The election was won handsomely by the Unionists, and partition did not subsequently feature in the Anglo-Irish discussions. The foundation in Northern Ireland of the Anti-Partition League in 1938 and its propaganda campaign in Britain was severely undermined by the IRA's activities in 1939–40, and the anti-partition campaign was dropped early in the Second World War. Similarly, the formation in 1945 of the Irish Anti-Partition League (supported by the British Labour Party's 'Friends of Ireland' campaign) had little effect in promoting discussion or debate on the Irish border either in Ireland or Britain. Despite its name, the League failed to develop a policy on how the Irish border should be removed. Indeed, it was the British Labour government that, in response to the passing of the Republic of Ireland Act in Dublin in 1948, responded with the Ireland Act of 1949, guaranteeing Northern Ireland's status as part of the United Kingdom unless and until the Northern Ireland parliament decided otherwise. Compared with the magnitude of earlier Irish political turbulence, all of this was merely an irritant to the British body politic, extraneous to it, not integral. Above all, nothing was to be said or done that could result in the Irish border, and all the historical baggage that went with it, returning to the heart of British political life. Discussion of the border in Britain was to be avoided at all costs.

In 1939 de Valera declared Irish neutrality in the Second World War in order to avoid invasion (by either the United Kingdom or Germany), to stress Irish sovereignty and to avoid reinvigorating old civil war and anti-British sentiments. The declaration of Irish neutrality, as controversial as it was, did not preclude Irish acquiescence in British military use of the waters and airspace of the contested Lough Foyle estuary and overflying of the Donegal Corridor by British seaplanes travelling west from Fermanagh in Northern Ireland to patrol the North Atlantic. An offer from Britain to end partition if Ireland entered the war on the allied side was treated cautiously by de Valera when it was revealed that the proposal would have to involve the support of the government of Northern Ireland, which was unlikely to be forthcoming.

Neither the IRA's ineffective border campaign of the 1950s nor the far more murderous Troubles that were sustained over a thirty-year period in the late twentieth century involved any realistic reconsideration of a possible realignment or removal of the border, despite both campaigns having the express ambition of removing the border permanently. In 1973, after violence in Northern Ireland had reached horrific proportions, the Conservative government in the United Kingdom undertook a border referendum in Northern Ireland. The outcome, which was substantially in favour of retention, was critically undermined by the nationalist decision to boycott the whole process. The Heath government in the early 1970s and Margaret Thatcher's government in the 1980s both considered (Heath while contemplating a doomsday scenario in the event of communal civil war) the feasibility of transferring nationalist areas and their populations to the Republic of Ireland. In both cases the idea was quickly dismissed as being impractical. It would have to involve widespread transfers of populations and a smaller but more Protestant Northern Ireland, which would, from a nationalist perspective, ironically have the opposite effect of what was desired: it would reinforce not weaken partition. In the 1990s, the idea arose again in a proposal by the Ulster Defence Association* that, in the event of British withdrawal from Northern Ireland, Catholic and nationalist areas of Northern Ireland were to be transferred to the Republic, with any nationalists remaining on the 'wrong' side of the redrawn border being expelled – or worse. Coming at the height of the Yugoslav Civil War and the systematic ethnic cleansing that was taking place, this proposal was universally condemned.

It is easy to see why such suggestions have been rejected by successive British (and Irish) governments. Not only would they have been highly controversial but they would also have raised the complexity of Irish politics being introduced into

---

*The largest loyalist paramilitary organisation in Northern Ireland.

mainstream British politics once again. Marginal transfers of population, while perhaps desirable in themselves, would have made no substantial impact on the underlying problem. In any event, no such transfers could have taken place under international law without the consent of those involved. More substantial transfers and exchanges of population would have been extremely difficult to achieve and might have resulted only in the creation of two sets of embittered refugees.

Although in the Anglo-Irish Agreement of 1985* there was provision for the establishment of a united Ireland if clearly indicated by the people of Northern Ireland that this was their wish, there was no further provision for a poll to determine the future constitutional status of Northern Ireland until the Good Friday Agreement and subsequent Northern Ireland Act of 1998. This allowed the British Secretary of State for Northern Ireland to hold such a poll no more frequently than once every seven years if it appeared that a majority of those voting were likely to vote in favour of a united Ireland. Article 3 of the Constitution of Ireland was subsequently amended to allow for a similar poll in the Republic, so that both jurisdictions would be able to vote.

As a result of the referendum in June 2016 rejecting the United Kingdom's continued membership of the European Union, the future of partition in Ireland is now regarded as being indissolubly linked to the future relationship between

---

* This Treaty between the United Kingdom and the Republic of Ireland aimed to end the Troubles in Northern Ireland and gave the Irish government an advisory role in Northern Ireland's government while guaranteeing the current constitutional position of Northern Ireland. It was opposed by Ulster unionists and loyalists.

the United Kingdom and the EU. During the debate over the backstop proposal, some nationalist politicians in both parts of Ireland argued that because Northern Ireland voted to stay inside the EU this increased the likelihood of a growth in support for ending partition and so sought to invoke the border poll component of the Good Friday Agreement. The argument now was that Northern Ireland had become a semi-detached part of the United Kingdom as a result of efforts to ensure that both the EU customs union and single market were maintained in Ireland, irrespective of the border. The solution to the backstop controversy – which effectively shifted the economic rather than the political border to the Irish Sea, thus magnifying the disparity between Northern Ireland and the rest of the United Kingdom to an even greater extent – has only increased demands for the implementation of a border poll to decide the future of partition. But the Irish border existed well before the 2016 referendum, and there is every expectation that it will survive long after the current Brexit controversy is resolved. Those calling for a border poll now are doing so with the expectation that significant numbers of the unionist middle class, appalled at the prospect of leaving the European Union, will vote to join the south to preserve their EU citizenship at the expense of their unionism. This is hardly a realistic assumption given the lessons and experience of the past hundred years. Arguably the greatest threat to the continuation of partition is demographic change in favour of Catholics over Protestants in Northern Ireland and the ongoing myopia on the part of some Ulster Protestants to make Northern Ireland anything but a 'cold house' for Catholics – in the famous words of former Ulster Unionist leader David Trimble.* A prime mitigating factor in favour of the retention of partition is undeniably the economic one, whereby the United Kingdom subvents Northern Ireland to the tune of £12 billion per year, and east–west trade between Northern Ireland and Britain outweighs north–south trade within Ireland by a margin of four to one. Recent economic predictions indicate that in the event of reunification the quickest and, arguably, only way to make up the subvention shortfall – as the Irish taxpayer is unlikely to manage it – is the immediate removal of forty thousand public service jobs from the Northern Irish economy. Undoubtedly, over time it would be possible to mitigate the worst financial effects of Irish reunification, but this would be at the cost of extended tax increases and spending cuts over a lengthy period – a seemingly permanent feature of Irish economic life that would somewhat detract from the promised attractions of the end of partition.

The likelihood is that the future of partition in Ireland will be determined not by Europe but by the same atavistic impulses in Northern Ireland that led to its establishment in the first place. Neither society, north or south, has made any sustained effort to promote their political project as an attractive proposition to those adopting an alternative position. This is even more relevant now that the Good Friday Agreement and the proposed border referendum are the only mechanisms whereby constitutional change can take place. Neither sovereign state has the power to accept or reject groups of people other than with the expressed majority will

---

* Nobel Lecture, 10 December 1998, Oslo.

of the populations in both jurisdictions. It follows, therefore, that a state such as the United Kingdom, even if it wanted to, could not legally expel up to a million of its citizens against their will. Equally, the Republic of Ireland could not accept the reunification of the country, even if Northern Ireland willed it, if its own citizens rejected this option in a separate southern referendum.

In summary, the expectation on the part of those people who want to see the end of partition in Ireland is that the uncertainty caused by Brexit in relation to Northern Ireland's constitutional position in the United Kingdom, allied to the impact of sustained demographic change in Northern Ireland, now makes the end of partition more likely and thus justifies the triggering of the border referendum element of the Good Friday Agreement and the subsequent Northern Ireland Act. In this, Sinn Féin and others interpret the agreement as a process that sooner or later will deliver the Holy Grail of a united Ireland. Unionists, however, see the agreement as a final settlement, and many believe that such polls should be fixed and generational.

It follows that if Irish nationalists wish to remove the border they will have to persuade Ulster unionists to agree to do so. As it stands, a simple majority of one vote would mark the end of partition. However, many observers on both sides question whether it is possible or desirable to formulate a fundamentally changed constitutional system without taking the time and energy to construct building blocks that would improve the chances of the new edifice thriving – or at least surviving. Past attempts to construct new political structures in Northern Ireland without consent do not suggest that future attempts will fare any better. In the not-too-distant past, Irish republicans expected sympathetic British politicians, particularly in the British Labour Party, to do their convincing for them by becoming proxy persuaders for Irish unity. If one accepts that unionists are unlikely to be convinced by a supposedly reformed version of the same kind of militant republicanism that they have experienced recently, the process must involve more Irish nationalists than just traditional republicans. A very real problem is which form of Irish nationalism unionists are expected to deal with. Sinn Féin is hardly anybody's idea of what a modern republican party is meant to be as expressed in the wider European world. In fact, most modern Irish nationalist parties have been more similar to Catholic separatist parties than truly secular republican parties. Irish republicans exchanged British colonialist imperialism for native Catholic imperialism while paying lip service to the traditions of Enlightenment European republicanism in their ranks, such as the United Irish tradition. Furthermore, Irish republican political movements were not always republican. Apart from the Fenian Brotherhood, whose use of recklessly violent tactics made them politically unsupportable, Sinn Féin was not initially a republican party nor was it, as late as 1921 according to its leader Éamon de Valera, a party of 'republican doctrinaires'. Its first leader, Arthur Griffith, argued for the restoration of a form of Home Rule based upon the Dual Monarchy of Britain and Ireland of 1782 to 1800 presided over by King George III and, as late as 1926, vice-president of the Irish Free State, Kevin O'Higgins, proposed the same. Sinn Féin never became an overtly republican party until 1917 so that Irish and, later, Ulster unionists were never sure which ideological variety of Irish nationalists they were confronted with. What they were more certain of was that they were against any weakening of the constitutional link between Ireland (and later Ulster) and the United Kingdom. In addition, modern independent Ireland was not always a sovereign state that Ulster could determine whether or not to join. Under the Government of Ireland Act of 1920, Southern Ireland was yet another integral part of the United Kingdom like Wales or Scotland; then from 1922 to 1937 it became a Dominion of the British Empire, was in an indeterminate, constitutionally uncertain position between 1937 and 1949 and finally became a fully fledged republic in 1949. In the words of James Chichester-Clark, prime minister of Northern Ireland, 1969–71: 'The border was never intended, on our part, as a major international frontier, an emerald curtain. It was others who piled brick upon brick along that wall so we could scarcely see or comprehend one another.'* The basic issue facing nationalist Ireland is whether it prizes total independence and sovereignty on the one hand or national unity on the other because, as recent history indicates, it seems impossible to have both given northern unionist intransigence on the former.

The core problem that Irish nationalists face is their complete inability to see any role for Britishness in modern Ireland and, as a result, consequent antagonism towards unionism and its allied links to Britain being considered a valid political philosophy in Ireland. Behind the veneer of fashionable

---

* Harvey, Brian et al., *The Emerald Curtain: The Social Impact of the Irish Border* (Carrickmacross: Triskele Community Training and Development, 2005).

inclusivity (particularly in Sinn Féin) Irish nationalists can sometimes exhibit a remarkably illiberal anti-Britishness which, if it were applied to other identities in Ireland, would be regarded as backward, bigoted and unacceptable. Inevitably, this means that any attempts at being republican persuaders for Irish unity are compromised. However, Sinn Féin does not own the blueprint for a united Ireland, and other Irish nationalists have a role to play – although they seem reluctant to step up to the plate, perhaps because they also have great difficulty in realising that the only solution to this never-ending conundrum that will appease (some or enough) unionists is some kind of institutional relationship with the United Kingdom.

Irish nationalism was born in the late nineteenth century as part of the rise in nationalism throughout Europe at that time. The idea that 'the people' was a single unit defined by its cultural and linguistic distinctiveness and entitled to its God-given 'natural' territory is only now being challenged in post-nationalist Ireland. This concept of nationalism also defined itself by what it was not – in Ireland's case, British. Other national entities in Europe resolved the problem of recalcitrant minorities, particularly in the mayhem of continental Europe after the First World War, by expulsion and forced transfers of populations. This did not happen on anything like the European scale in Ireland, although there was substantial Protestant flight from the south to both Northern Ireland and Britain after 1922 as well as Catholic refugees fleeing Belfast and east Ulster between 1920 and 1922. In Ireland, a long-established older philosophy of secular republicanism, theoretically uniting Irish people irrespective of religious affiliation, gave cover to the same ethnic nationalism prevalent in Europe after the First World War.

The new Irish state, however, was not based upon modern, secular, truly republican beliefs but largely on an earlier model of nineteenth-century principles of national identity – exclusivist, Catholic, Gaelic and rural – rather than the democratic, inclusive, secular Enlightenment principles of the United States and France. It was perhaps inevitable after such a lengthy period under British domination that the new state was to base its identity on what it meant to be Irish, on those characteristics that were the opposite of being British. However, the effect was to further alienate the one-fifth of the population that defined itself as the very opposite that was anathema to Irish nationalism. If Irish unionists rejected more moderate and pragmatic nationalists such as the Home Rulers, they were hardly likely to be attracted to the more purist and ideological nationalists who often identified their nationalism, in part at least, in terms of not being British.

For most of the twentieth century, Irish nationalists hardly made any attempt to reconcile their version of Ireland with the unionists' version. The old nostrums did start to break down after 1973 when the south began to embrace the social and economic secularism that came with joining the European Economic Community. However, there has been little real effort on the part of nationalist Ireland to break out of its former cosy homogeneity and relative political tranquillity in a sustained attempt to attract northern unionists. This is perhaps surprising given that the ethnic, religious and linguistic conformity and homogeneity that characterised the southern state for most of its existence has itself now been transformed into a vibrant modern multiculturalism. That multiculturalism, though, seems not to include the British-ness that has been such a feature of Irishness for so long; indeed, embracing Britishness seems to be a step too far. This is unfortunate given the historical, linguistic, social, cul-tural and economic links that have bound the two countries together over the lengthy history of their relationship. There seems to be little enthusiasm for the need, for example, to craft a brand-new constitution for a post-partitionist Ireland. The central question has to be what, if anything, would national-ist Ireland give up for a united country? A unified all-Ireland state would inevitably comprise two national identities and would have to be built from the ground up rather than have one part of Ireland grafted on to an existing state, as happened after the reunification of East and West Germany in 1990. At the very least, the new constitution would have to provide formal recognition of symbols of Britishness in the new Irish state. In particular, symbols such as the monarchy and the Commonwealth provide tangible reminders of a British con-nection out of all proportion to what they practically achieve. The Commonwealth is often regarded as a nostalgic relic, but its fifty-four states (thirty-three of which are republics) with a population of 2.4 billion theoretically offer a new Ireland an opportunity to extend its influence hugely – particularly to those states such as Canada, Australia and New Zealand where so many Irish people, from both north and south, have made new lives. The new Irish state would at the very least require a freshly drafted constitution to recognise the additional cul-tural, religious and political values of its new citizens, thus rejecting the tenets of an eighty-year-old constitution that reflected the nature of an almost exclusively Catholic state. A new head of state would have to be considered as would, possibly, a new capital city, a new national flag and a new national anthem. Would the new state be a highly centralised one as is the current case, or would Ulster have devolved responsibilities? We could easily be back to the debates of a century ago whereby Irish nationalists were prepared to accommodate any amount of devolution for Ulster as long as the 'essential integrity' of Ireland was recognised. Would any amount of devolution to the north be offered to the other provinces as well, and, given the cultural homogeneity of the rest of Ireland, would it be justified? Would a self-governing Ulster consist of six or nine counties, and would it be a version of the current power-sharing structure devolved this time from Dublin (or elsewhere in Ireland) rather than London? Would the rest of Ireland and, in particular, nationalists in Northern Ireland accept what could be interpreted as a unionist-dominated federal province?

Then again, would the effort of devising a new constitution be worth it? The political and cultural impact of partitionism in the south has been alluring to many, as it allowed a homogenously coherent society to be introduced, particularly in the early years of the new state's existence. Creating another new state would undoubtedly create substantial controversy, with the prospect of very little return if northern unionists were to reject it. Many nationalists may insist upon a referendum without considering fundamental change to the southern state, particularly if it were apparent that northern unionists were simply not interested in forsaking a unionism which, by definition, meant continued union with the United Kingdom.

In asking unionists to give up the union, are Irish nationalists prepared to make their own sacrifices for the unity of Ireland? And how many citizens of the south would even contemplate making such radical constitutional changes on the off-chance that sufficient numbers of unionists could be attracted to the concept of a united Ireland? The Republic of Ireland is currently a totally sovereign state. One of the obvious ways of recognising Ireland's British connection is for a constitutional reconnection between Britain and Ireland. However, given the tortuous process through which Ireland asserted its sovereignty, particularly in the first thirty years of its existence, it is highly unlikely that the state would meekly offer back that same sovereignty, which was so assertively fought for and won. This is exactly the same question that dominated the Anglo-Irish Treaty debates in Dublin nearly a century ago, and it is still as controversial and uncomfortable now as it was then. It is depressing that after nearly a century of independence Irish nationalism still lacks sufficient self-confidence to interpret emblems of Britishness – membership of the Commonwealth, for example – as anything other than a threat. India, which became independent a quarter of a century after Ireland and whose founding fathers derived so much inspiration from Ireland's example, does not see membership of the Commonwealth as endangering its republican principles, nor is it motivated by a negative Anglophobia in the way that much of nationalist Ireland is still. The conclusion can only be that Irish nationalists' outreach to their separated brethren in the north is still very much a work in progress.

Equally, Ulster unionists will have to reach out to their nationalist fellow citizens in the north if they want to ensure that partition survives much beyond its centenary. The border was established to ensure a permanent Protestant and union-ist majority in the new state. British politics may have moved on and the old civil-war politics may have disappeared even in the south, but the central political issue in Northern Ireland remains the same as it was a century ago. At that time there was no incentive, not the slightest inclination, to attract reluc-tant Catholics to the new state. The disdain and contempt shown towards their fellow citizens by the Northern Ireland political leadership in the formative years of the state's exist-ence only compounded the issue and sowed dragons' teeth, which resulted in the destruction of the unionist administra-tion forty years later. Today, 45 per cent of the population is from a Catholic background, and they have not forgotten the rejection of their community throughout the past century of a Northern Ireland state. The demographic picture of the early years of Northern Ireland has now dramatically changed through the increased Catholic birth rate and the flight to Britain of the university-educated Protestant middle class. With delicious piquancy, the number of Catholics in North-ern Ireland is predicted to equal the number of Protestants in 2021, the same year that partition reaches its centenary. However, it has been conjectured that if Catholics become numerically dominant it might be an attractive proposi-tion for them to vote in any future border poll to remain in the union where they would now be in the majority while at the same time being able to continue to take advantage of the superior public services compared with the south – so predictions that the future of partition will depend on a straightforward sectarian headcount may be wide of the mark.

From a unionist perspective, in order for the border to remain there has to be a move from an ethnic to a civic unionism and an active appeal to Catholics to support the union. Depressingly, many unionists seem thus far to have been largely reticent in reaching out to argue their case to non-unionists. The recent Brexit backstop controversy undoubtedly provided an impetus for proposals based on all-Ireland structures, including, of course, the removal of partition and the establishment of a united Ireland. Now that pro-Brexit unionists have been wrong-footed and the all-Ireland economy would seem to be based on a border in the Irish Sea rather than along the line of partition, does that help or hinder the prospects for a united Ireland more than the previous Brexit conundrum? Irrespective of the changing nature of the threat facing unionists as a result of the shifting Brexit problem, most appear not to be prepared to countenance the likely threat facing their political position based on Brexit and changing demographics or, if they do, to enter into debate and discussion on negotiations, timescales and means of reaching agreements – if, in fact, Brexit makes a poll on the future of the border any more likely. Having said that, there is at least some evidence that progressive and far-sighted unionists are prepared to argue for agreed cross-community processes and timetables to be established for the future governance of Northern Ireland (and indeed Ireland) rather than continually fixating on the immediate controversies that separate the communities and perpetuate political crisis.

So the final question remains: will partition in Ireland survive? In 1912, the idea that within a decade a border would be dividing Ireland into two states would have been (and was) treated with incredulity. Even the most ardent unionist supporter of partition in 1921 could not have contemplated that the border would still be in existence a century later. It was expected that partition was a temporary arrangement to help overcome an immediate political crisis. Unionists could (and did) always point out that Ireland has only ever been united under British rule and that the political reunification of Ireland could surely be achieved as part of a new constitutional arrangement between Britain and Ireland. However, after a hundred years of Irish independence, the prospects of the Republic of Ireland joining a federation of the two countries, as has been suggested by some unionist and British Conservative commentators, seems somewhat remote – even if federation could end Irish partition and facilitate the reunification of Ireland.

The credit or blame (depending on one's perspective) for the existence of the Irish border must be shared by all British political parties as well as by the competing nationalisms in Ireland. A border that was originally a county boundary is now an international border, and, although intended to be temporary, it still remains. According to the Good Friday Agreement, this border can only be removed by the democratic will of the electorate operating in both parts of Ireland, with that will being expressed no more than once every seven years. Currently there is little evidence to suggest that the Irish border will disappear with the same alacrity that the German border did in 1990; and, indeed, after thirty years of a united Germany the mental and psychological border between east and west remains. The Irish border has been in existence for a century – more than twice the length of time the German border existed. In addition, it was not imposed peremptorily from outside, against the wishes of a unified nation, as was the case in Germany. The appearance of a partitioned Ireland in 1921 reflected centuries of cultural, ethnic and religious differences, and it would be unrealistic to expect that if partition were removed the same psychological separateness would not continue to be experienced between the two parts of Ireland for decades to come. The significance, as well as the psychological impact of the border, should not be underestimated; it symbolised certainty and security for the unionist majority within. However, because of this majority's inability and unwillingness to welcome their nationalist neighbours as equal citizens, that same border became a symbol of discrimination and a constant reminder to nationalists of their second-class status.

Paradoxically, it was by benefiting from the advanced social and educational standards of the British welfare state as extended to Northern Ireland that the nationalist population came to no longer tolerate this status. This was evidenced by the growth of a substantial Catholic middle class that expected to be treated as equal citizens in Northern Ireland and first manifested dramatically in the late 1960s with the birth of the civil rights movement. The concept of equality that emerged then (known as 'parity of esteem') became, thirty years later, the cornerstone of the Good Friday Agreement. For the first fifty years of Northern Ireland's existence, it was in the political and economic interests of both states to maintain a secure border. This security aspect intensified during the Troubles of the late twentieth century even as, paradoxically, the economic necessity of the border dissolved with the arrival of the

European Single Market. Following the Good Friday Agreement in 1998 – and for over twenty years – there has been no visible Irish border. Prior to the recent Brexit controversies there was evidence that, because of greater equality, increased prosperity and the availability of more sophisticated public services in Northern Ireland, now all in a post-Good Friday Agreement political climate, more Catholics in Northern Ireland were becoming reconciled to their position inside the United Kingdom. This may still be the case; however, reluctance to accept the constitutional status quo may have increased as a result of continued Brexit uncertainty, and the potential loss of EU citizenship (although, as Irish passport holders, Northern Irish people can remain EU citizens) and traditional affinity with the south may persuade more nationalists in Northern Ireland to vote for Irish unity than would otherwise be the case. This will only become apparent if a poll on the future of the border takes place. However, whether or not Ireland remains partitioned is now out of the hands of politicians, diplomats and boundary commissioners and can only be determined by the electorates in both parts of Ireland agreeing on its future.

Suggested Further Reading

Bew, Paul, Peter Gibbon and Henry Patterson, *Northern Ireland 1921–1994* (London 1995)

Bowman, John, *De Valera and the Ulster Question 1917–73* (Oxford: Oxford University Press, 1989)

Boyce, D. G., *The Irish Question and British Politics 1868–1996* (London: Palgrave, 1996)

Buckland, Patrick, *James Craig* (Dublin: Gill and Macmillan, 1980)

Collins, Peter (ed.), *Nationalism and Unionism: Conflict in Ireland 1885–1921* (Belfast: Institute of Irish Studies, 1994)

Ferriter, Diarmaid, *The Border: The Legacy of a Century of Anglo-Irish Politics* (London: Profile, 2019)

Fitzpatrick, David, *The Two Irelands: 1912–1939* (Oxford: Oxford University Press, 1998)

Gibbons, Ivan, *The British Labour Party and the Establishment of the Irish Free State 1918–1924* (Basingstoke: Palgrave, 2015)

Hand, Geoffrey J. (ed.), *Report of the Irish Boundary Commission 1925* (Dublin: Irish University Press, 1969)

Harkness, D. W., *Northern Ireland Since 1920* (Dublin: Helicon 1983)

Harvey, Brian et al., *The Emerald Curtain: The Social Impact of the Irish Border* (Carrickmacross: Triskele Community Training and Development, 2005)

Hennessey, Thomas, *A History of Northern Ireland 1920–1996* (Dublin: Gill and Macmillan, 1997)

Hennessey, Thomas, *Dividing Ireland: World War One and Partition* (London: Routledge, 1998)

Jones, Thomas (ed. Keith Middlemas), *Whitehall Diary, Vol. 3, Ireland 1918–1925* (Oxford: Oxford University Press, 1971)

Kennedy, Dennis, *The Widening Gulf: Northern Attitudes to the Independent Irish State 1919–49* (Belfast: Blackstaff Press, 1988)

Kenny, Mary, *Crown and Shamrock: Love and Hate Between Ireland and the British Monarchy* (Dublin: New Island Books, 2009)

Laffan, Michael, *The Partition of Ireland 1911–1925* (Dublin: Dundalgan Press, 1983)

Lee, J. J., *Ireland 1912–1985: Politics and Society* (Cambridge: Cambridge University Press, 1989)

Lynch, Robert, *The Partition of Ireland 1918–1925* (Cambridge: Cambridge University Press, 2019)

Matthews, Kevin, *Fatal Influence: The Impact of Ireland on British Politics 1920–1925* (Dublin: University College Dublin Press, 2004)

McGarry, John and Brendan O'Leary, *Explaining Northern Ireland* (Oxford: Wiley-Blackwell, 1995)

Moore, Cormac, *Birth of the Border: The Impact of Partition in Ireland* (Dublin: Merrion Press, 2019)

Murray, Paul, *The Irish Boundary Commission and its Origins 1886–1925* (Dublin: University College Dublin Press, 2011)

O'Day, Alan, *Irish Home Rule 1867–1921* (Manchester: Manchester University Press, 1998)

O'Halloran, Clare, *Partition and the Limits of Irish Nationalism: An Ideology Under Stress* (Dublin: Gill and Macmillan, 1987)

Phoenix, Eamon, *Northern Nationalism: Nationalist Politics, Partition and the Catholic Minority in Northern Ireland 1890–1940* (Belfast: Ulster Historical Foundation, 1994)

Staunton, Enda, *The Nationalists of Northern Ireland 1918–1973* (Dublin: Columba Press, 2001)

Chronology

1800	Act of Union creates United Kingdom of Great Britain and Ireland
1829	Catholic Relief Act (the culmination of Catholic Emancipation grants full civil liberties to Irish and British Roman Catholics)
1845–49	Great Famine
1886	Gladstone's First Home Rule Bill rejected in House of Commons
1893	Gladstone's Second Home Rule Bill rejected in House of Lords
1898	Irish Local Government Act democratises Irish local politics
1912–14	Third Home Rule Bill becomes law; enactment postponed for duration of First World War
1916	Easter Rising: Irish republican insurrection in Dublin
1918	Sinn Féin victory in general election
1919–21	Anglo-Irish War: guerrilla warfare in Ireland between British forces and IRA
1920	Government of Ireland Act partitions Ireland
1921	Northern Ireland and Irish border created
1921	Anglo-Irish Treaty establishes the Irish Free State

1922	Northern Ireland opts out of the Irish Free State, triggering the Boundary Commission to review border delineation
1922–23	Irish Civil War in response to Anglo-Irish Treaty: conflict between pro- and anti-Treaty republicans
1925	Boundary Commission report suppressed; Irish border remains unchanged
1932–38	Economic War, or the Anglo-Irish Trade War, between Britain and the Irish Free State
1939	IRA campaign in Britain
1939	Irish neutrality declared in the Second World War
1945	Irish Anti-Partition League established
1948	Republic of Ireland declared
1949	British government confirms Northern Ireland's status in the United Kingdom via the Ireland Act
1956–62	IRA border campaign in Northern Ireland
1969	Northern Ireland conflict (the Troubles) commences
1998	Good Friday Agreement ends Northern Ireland conflict
2016	Brexit referendum; Northern Ireland votes to remain inside European Union
2021	Centenary of the establishment of Northern Ireland

Dramatis Personae

Thomas Agar-Robartes	Liberal MP for St Austell 1908–15; proposed partition of Ireland in an amendment to Third Home Rule Bill 1912
Herbert Asquith	British Liberal Prime Minister 1908–16
Stanley Baldwin	British Conservative Prime Minister 1923–4, 1924–9; National Government Prime Minister 1935–7
Arthur Balfour	Chief Secretary for Ireland 1887–91; British Conservative Prime Minister 1902–5
Lord Birkenhead (F. E. Smith)	Lord Chancellor in Lloyd George's coalition government 1919–22; leading British negotiator on the Anglo-Irish Treaty
Augustine Birrell	Liberal Chief Secretary for Ireland 1907–16; resigned after Easter Rising
Ernest Blythe	Irish Free State Minister for Finance 1923–32 and Vice-President of the Executive Council of the Irish Free State 1927–32

Andrew Bonar Law Leader of the British Conservative
Party 1911–21, 1922–3; Prime Minister
1922–3

Sir Basil Brooke Organised unionist paramilitaries
in Co. Fermanagh in 1920; Prime
Minister of Northern Ireland 1943–63

Sir Edward Leader of the Ulster Unionist Party
Carson 1910–21; British War Cabinet member
1915, 1916–18

Austen Son of Joseph Chamberlain;
Chamberlain Conservative Party leader in Lloyd
George's coalition government 1921–2

Joseph Liberal Unionist politician opposed to
Chamberlain Irish Home Rule

Lord Randolph Father of Winston Churchill; British
Churchill Conservative politician opposed to the
1886 First Home Rule Bill

Winston Secretary of State for the Colonies in
Churchill Lloyd George's coalition government
1921–2; British negotiator for the
Anglo-Irish Treaty 1921

Tom Clarke Fenian and leader of Irish Republican
Brotherhood; leader of the Easter
Rising; executed in 1916

Michael Collins Irish republican leader; chairman of
the Provisional Government of the
Irish Free State from January 1922
until his assassination in August 1922

William T. Cosgrave	First President of the Executive Council of the Irish Free State, 1922–32
Sir James Craig	Ulster Unionist leader and First Prime Minister of Northern Ireland, 1921–40
Joseph Devlin	Irish Parliamentary Party MP 1902–21; Northern Ireland Nationalist MP 1921–34
Richard Feetham	South African High Court Judge; Chairman of the Irish Boundary Commission 1924–5
J. R. Fisher	Former editor of the *Northern Whig*; appointed Northern Ireland representative on the Irish Boundary Commission
Garret FitzGerald	Leader of the Fine Gael Party and Taoiseach 1981–2, 1982–7
William Gladstone	British Liberal Prime Minister 1868–74, 1880–5, 1886, 1892–4
Arthur Griffith	Founder of Sinn Féin; Irish negotiator for the Anglo-Irish Treaty; President of Dáil Éireann from January 1922 until his death in August 1922
Edward Heath	British Conservative Prime Minister 1970–4
Arthur Henderson	Labour Home Secretary 1924; Secretary of State for Foreign Affairs 1929–31
David Lloyd George	British Liberal Prime Minister 1916–22

Lord Londonderry (Charles Vane-Tempest Stewart)	Northern Ireland Minister for Education 1921–6
Walter Long	Leader of Irish Unionist Alliance 1906–10; initiator of Irish partition in the Government of Ireland Act 1920
Ramsay MacDonald	British Labour Prime Minister 1924, 1929–31; National Government Prime Minister 1931–5
Eoin MacNeill	Irish Free State Minister for Education 1922–5; Irish Free State Boundary Commissioner 1924–5
General Nevil Macready	General Officer Commander-in-Chief of British forces in Ireland 1920; organised counter-insurgency role against the IRA
Thomas S. McAllister	Northern Ireland Nationalist MP 1925–9
Daniel O'Connell, 'The Liberator'	Political leader of Ireland's Roman Catholic majority; secured Catholic Emancipation in 1829
Jeremiah O'Donovan Rossa	Irish Fenian leader and member of the Irish Republican Brotherhood
Kevin O'Higgins	Irish Free State Minister for Justice 1922–7; Vice-President of the Executive Council of the Irish Free State 1922–7; assassinated by the IRA in 1927

Kevin O'Shiel	Assistant Legal Advisor to Irish Free State government 1922–3; Director of North Eastern Boundary Bureau 1922–5
Patrick Pearse	Republican activist and leader of the Easter Rising; executed 1916
William Pitt the Younger	British Prime Minister 1783–1801, 1804–6
John Redmond	Leader of the Irish Parliamentary Party 1900–18
Lord Salisbury (Robert Gascoyne-Cecil)	British Conservative Prime Minister 1885–6, 1886–92, 1895–1902
Jan Smuts	Boer War military leader; Prime Minister of the Union of South Africa 1919–24, 1939–48
Charles Stewart Parnell	Leader of the Irish Parliamentary Party 1882–91
Margaret Thatcher	British Conservative Prime Minister 1979–90
J. H. Thomas	Labour Secretary of State for the Colonies 1924, Secretary of State for Dominion Affairs 1930–5; regarded as the Labour spokesperson on Ireland
David Trimble	Leader of the Ulster Unionist Party 1995–2005; First Minister of Northern Ireland 1998–2002

Sir Henry Tudor   Chief of Police in Ireland; introduced Black and Tan and Auxiliary support to the Royal Irish Constabulary in 1920

Éamon de Valera   Anti-Treaty Irish republican leader; President of the Executive Council of the Irish Free State 1932–7; Taoiseach 1937–48, 1951–4, 1957–9; President of Ireland 1959–73

Sir Henry Wilson   Chief of the Imperial General Staff 1918–22; Security Advisor to Northern Ireland government 1921–2; Unionist MP for North Down 1921; assassinated by the IRA in June 1922

George Wyndham   Conservative Chief Secretary for Ireland 1900–5; author of the Irish Land Act 1903

Index

A

Agar-Robartes, Thomas 34–5
Anderson, John 64
Antrim 34, 39, 64
Armagh 34, 39, 99–100, 106, 113
Asquith, H. H. 7–9, 27–8, 34, 37,
    39, 41–2, 47, 84
Australia 7, 29, 67, 72, 143

B

Bailey, W. F. 47–8
Baldwin, Stanley 14, 81–2, 85,
    90–4, 99, 117, 119–20, 131
Balfour, Arthur 32, 54
Banbridge 111–13
Belfast 5, 20, 31–2, 36, 39,
    57–8, 59, 62–6, 93, 95, 102–3,
    108, 112–15, 118–19, 121, 123–4,
    141
Bessbrook 111–13, 115
Birkenhead, Lord 91
Birrell, Augustine 47–8
Blythe, Ernest 11
Bonar Law, Andrew 24, 29, 32–3,
    40–1, 81–2, 84, 91–2
Brooke, Sir Basil 64

C

Camlough 111
Canada 3, 5, 7, 29, 67, 72, 143
Cardiff 6
Carlingford Lough 97, 112, 114
Carson, Sir Edward 7, 32–3,
    35–40, 42, 54
Castleknock 15
Cavan 48, 107
Chamberlain, Austen 91
Chamberlain, Joseph 5, 20
Churchill, Lord Randolph 9
Churchill, Winston 44, 64,
    126–7, 131
Clarke, Tom 26
Co. Donegal *see* Donegal
Co. Londonderry *see*
    Londonderry
Collins, Michael 60, 75, 84, 124
Cork 32, 63
Cosgrave, W. T. 85–7, 90, 102,
    117–120, 124–5
Craig, James 7, 12, 38, 59, 64–5,
    69, 76, 80, 83, 85, 87–8, 90, 93,
    101–2, 117, 119–22, 124, 127–30,
    132

Creeslough 21
Crossmaglen 111–12

D
Derry/Londonderry (city) 20, 48,
    62–4, 99–100, 106–11
    see also Londonderry (county)
de Valera, Éamon 13–14, 62,
    67, 70, 84, 124–5, 129, 131–3,
    139
Devlin, Joseph 12, 62, 122–4
Donegal 100, 106, 108–9
    Co. Donegal 21, 109
    corridor 133
    east 107, 109–11, 115–16
Dougherty, James B. 47
Down 34, 39, 100, 106–7, 112
    North Down 80
Downpatrick 107
Dublin 5, 13, 15–16, 19–20, 25,
    28–9, 31–3, 35, 37, 47, 64, 67,
    70–2, 80, 85, 86, 89, 95, 101,
    117–18, 121, 125, 132, 144–5
Dundalk 64, 108, 113
Dunfanaghy 22

E
East Donegal *see* Donegal
East Prussia 3
Edinburgh 5
Enniskillen 99–100

F
Falcarragh 22
Feetham, Richard 88–9, 97–9,
    101–6, 110, 119

Fermanagh 39–40, 44, 64, 68,
    100, 106, 110, 126, 133
Fisher, J. R. 90, 101–2
FitzGerald, Garret 26

G
Germany 2, 28, 34, 36, 68, 130,
    133, 143, 148–9
Gladstone, William 4–5, 21, 24,
    28, 35
Greenore 108, 113
Griffith, Arthur 68, 70, 124,
    139

H
Henderson, Arthur 51

I
India 3, 95, 145
Inishowen 111

K
Kilkeel 111–12
Killeter 107
Killyhevlin 100
Kingstown (Dun Laoghaire) 15
Knocknamoe 100

L
Lisburn 63–4
Lisnaskea 64
Lloyd George, David 6, 8–9, 27,
    39, 42–3, 50, 52–5, 59–60, 64,
    67–9, 73, 75, 77, 79, 81–2, 84,
    91–2, 96–7, 116–17, 119–20,
    131

Londonderry (county) 34, 39, 100, 106, 110–11
for the city, *see* Derry
Londonderry, Lord 12
Long, Walter 50, 52, 54
Lough Erne 100
Lough Foyle 97, 109, 111, 133

M
Macaulay, Lord 20
MacDonald, Ramsay 14, 92, 94, 101, 131
MacNeill, Eoin 85, 101, 106, 118
Macready, General Nevil 64
Magherafelt 107
McAllister, T. S. 123
Monaghan 48, 100, 106–7
Mourne Mountains 114
Moville 111

N
Newry 64, 100, 106–9, 112–16
Newtownstewart 99

O
O'Connell, Daniel 18, 20
O'Donovan Rossa, Jeremiah 26
O'Higgins, Kevin 118, 123–4, 139
Omagh 85, 100
O'Shiel, Kevin 85

P
Palestine 3, 95
Parnell, Charles Stewart 18, 20, 21, 23, 28

Pearse, Patrick 26
Pitt, William 16–17
Poland 2, 68
Portadown 108, 111–13, 115

R
Redmond, John 7, 23, 27, 40, 42
River Foyle 108
Robinson, Henry Augustus 47
Rostrevor 100

S
Salisbury, Marquess of 20, 28
Silesia 2–3, 68
Smuts, Jan 59
South Africa 3, 88
South Armagh 96, 107, 112, 116
Stormont x, 12, 46
Strabane 48, 100, 109–10

T
Thomas, J. H. 51
Tirconnail (Donegal) 106
Tudor, Sir Henry 64
Tyrone 39–40, 44, 68, 99–100, 106–7, 110, 126

W
Warrenpoint 108, 111
Wilson, Henry 64, 80

Y
Yugoslavia 134